First-aid and
for your

First-aid
and Nursing
for your Dog

F. Andrew Edgson
M.R.C.V.S.

and

Olwen Gwynne-Jones

POPULAR DOGS
London   Melbourne   Auckland   Johannesburg

Popular Dogs Publishing Co. Ltd

An imprint of Century Hutchinson Ltd

Brookmount House, 62–65 Chandos Place,
Covent Garden, London WC2N 4NW

Century Hutchinson Australia (Pty) Ltd
PO Box 496, 16–22 Church Street, Hawthorn, Melbourne, Victoria 3122

Century Hutchinson New Zealand Limited
32–34 View Road, PO Box 40–086, Glenfield, Auckland 10

Century Hutchinson South Africa (Pty) Ltd
PO Box 337, Bergvlei 2012, South Africa

First published 1954
Revised editions 1959, 1962, 1968, 1973, 1975, 1979, 1982, 1987

Copyright © Popular Dogs Publishing Co. Ltd 1954, 1959, 1962, 1968, 1973, 1975,
1979, 1982, 1987

Set in Times by BookEns, Saffron Walden, Essex

Printed and bound in Great Britain by Anchor Brendon Limited, Tiptree, Essex

British Library Cataloguing in Publication Data

Edgson, F. Andrew
First-aid and nursing for your dog.
1. Dogs—Diseases 2. First aid for
animals
I. Title II. Gwynne-Jones, Olwen
636.7'08960252   SF991

ISBN 0 09 164771 1

Contents

Author's Foreword by F. Andrew Edgson

1 How to Handle your Dog in an
  Emergency   5

2 Some Principles of Canine Nursing   7

3 Index to Treatment and Care of
  Common Troubles   14

4 Recent Advances in Veterinary Surgery   80

  Appendix   84

  Index   86

Illustrations

PHOTOGRAPHS

(Between pages 44 and 45)

A dog with a plaster cast on a fractured leg

A steel pin inserted at a fracture of the humerus (a series of three radiographs)

A greyhound races with a plastic bone in her hock

IN THE TEXT

Figure 1	'Figure of eight' nose tie	6
Figure 2	The 'figure of eight' nose tie in position	6
Figure 3	A useful bed for sick puppies	9
Figure 4	Pattern for pneumonia jacket	58

Author's Foreword

The purposes of this short book are two. Firstly, to provide the dog owner with a guide for use in times of emergency. Secondly, how to care for and nurse the animal in a variety of conditions.

It is emphasised that first-aid measures are *not* the whole treatment for the conditions listed. It is hoped that by providing the dog owner with some knowledge of the correct action to take in emergencies, and in after-care, he will be able to give his animal practical help. Attention by a veterinary surgeon is essential in many of the conditions mentioned, and no attempt is made to discuss the specialised approach of the expert.

In the past, 'first-aid' has often done more harm than good, and aggravated rather than alleviated. Canine nursing and day-to-day care is essential for full and rapid recovery, a fact sometimes sadly neglected.

This guide has been made as comprehensive as possible, but its limitations are realised. It will not, of course, cover every emergency. In cases of doubt, where the right course may not be obvious, it is often best to do nothing until skilled help arrives.

It will be seen that in some instances no first-aid measures are advised; what to refrain from doing is advice equally, if not more, important.

Nursing measures and the care of the animal in convalescence have been included, as the authors felt that such knowledge is often lacking. It should not be necessary for the busy veterinary surgeon to have to explain in detail such simple measures as dosing, handling, etc. This aspect is dealt with by a dog breeder of experience, one who is fully conversant with practical difficulties and with the best ways to overcome them.

Common conditions and mishaps have been arranged alphabetically for easy reference. It is, however, best to make yourself conversant with the action to take in any emergency rather than have to refer to the book. This is vital in some circumstances, such as choking, when immediately available knowledge may save a dog's life, which might be lost if you have to read up what to do.

1954   F.A.E.

Since this book was first published in 1954, veterinary science has progressed further than the most optimistic of veterinary surgeons of the fifties could have hoped, and in all areas of treatment. In surgery for example new anaesthetic agents have made general anaesthetic a very safe procedure which has given the surgeon that most valuable commodity when operating – time. Animals can now be safely kept unconscious for longer periods to enable more detailed and delicate techniques to be successfully completed using the newer anaesthetic procedures.

In veterinary medicine, we now have a positive galaxy of antibiotics and chemotherapeutics each of which would have been hailed as a miracle cure thirty-two years ago.

Despite all these advances, in many circumstances the only person who can help is you. In accident or sudden illness, it is up to you to provide the first-aid and start the processes which will eventually restore your dog to full health. Knowledge of the first-aid and nursing procedures, we hope, will be of as much value today as it was in

1954.
1987   F.A.E.

1

How to Handle your Dog in an Emergency

Today we are faced with a new phenomenon – the anti-dog lobby, who attack the keeping of dogs as pets. Occasionally, they do have a point when dogs are allowed to roam loose, cause accidents and foul pavements. So a trained dog is not only a joy to have, but a friend of society and not a curse. The handling of a dog should start when he is a puppy, and simple lessons in obedience are good for the daily management of a dog, just as some degree of discipline is good for his owner. The properly trained and handled dog is not a cowed dog, but one who is a credit to his owner, and not a constant nuisance and irritation to others. Therefore simple obedience training, which the animal enjoys learning, is an important part of his education. Commands such as coming when called, sitting when told, and coming to heel at a word, are simple orders which should be impressed upon every dog. To own a dog is not only to care for it but to control it as well. If this truth were more widely recognised dogs would be less frequently subjected to criticism that should properly fall upon the owner. More important, accidents would be reduced, as it is usually the undisciplined dog which causes, or is involved in, accidents.

Control of a dog in an emergency is very important. The ability to apply any first-aid measures rapidly depends upon it. Many dogs, especially when in pain or shocked, resent efforts to help them. It is therefore important to be able to apply, quickly efficiently and firmly, methods of control as and when required. These measures are best carried out by the owner, as even the most frightened dog will usually heed a person he knows. Obviously any restraint should be carried out with minimum disturbance and as gently as possible, in order to avoid hurting or exciting the animal.

A collar should, of course, always be worn by your dog, this is a legal requirement. It is a useful means by which a dog can be caught if at all hysterical. A walking-stick slipped through it is the safest way if the dog appears vicious. Another useful method by which a dog of doubtful temperament can be caught is with the lead as a noose, the catch end being slipped through the hand loop and the noose then directed over the dog's head and tightened when actually over its neck. This can be done without handling the dog, or having the hands nearer than two or three feet to the animal, and is an excellent way of catching an hysterical or vicious dog.

Even the most disciplined dog will, if in pain, be inclined to snap, often unintentionally if hurt. Some control of the biting end can be obtained with a lead, tape, or bandage, as illustrated.

Figure 1
'Figure of eight' nose tie

This is merely a figure of eight, with one circle occupied by the nose, the other by the neck, on the back of which the knot is tied fairly firmly (Figure 2). This tie is more efficient if the nose piece is double in the form of a clove hitch, but this may require a little practice.

Whilst the importance of restraint cannot be overstressed, it is worth noting that taping of dogs is not often required; it is surprising how rarely this or some other restraint is necessary in veterinary practice. A firm but gentle hand on the scruff, and a few kind words, are usually all that are needed for the normal, educated dog, even when he is being subjected to measures he must naturally resent.

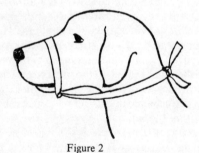

Figure 2
The 'figure of eight' nose tie in position

2

Some Principles of Canine Nursing

Few dogs pass through life without at least one illness during which the owner must give nursing care, and very often the animal's recovery or the reverse depends to a large extent on the quality of the attention he receives. Canine patients differ from humans in that they cannot be kept in bed unless they are too weak to get out, and their co-operation has to be obtained by persuasion rather than by request. A human patient will submit to the unpleasantness of constant intra-muscular injections of penicillin, for instance, because he knows it is for his own good, but a dog cannot be expected to reason in this way, and as some treatments given to sick dogs (inhalations, for example) are not welcomed by the patient the attendant may have a difficult time. On the whole, however, dogs – even very young ones – make good patients provided they have confidence in their nurse and, not less important, in the veterinary surgeon. If a dog trusts his attendant he submits with quite good grace and often astonishing resignation and stoicism to many unpleasant measures, and even shows gratitude in a touching fashion.

When an animal is sufficiently ill to require nursing he should be put in a separate room or kennel, even if the malady is not infectious. The general hubbub of the kitchen or living-room is not restful, and every sick animal needs plenty of sleep and peace. This is particularly the case with distemper and hard-pad – some dogs spend most of their time sleeping during the early stages of the former – and, in addition, the nervous system is often affected in both diseases and a noisy, restless environment may result in the dreaded distemper or hard-pad fits.

Much will depend on the time of year whether the dog is allowed out to relieve himself or not. If possible, house-trained dogs should always be taken out for this purpose (if necessary wearing a coat and on a lead to prevent undue excitement or exertion) as a very clean dog will suffer if forced to 'misbehave' indoors. In hot summer weather the dog is probably better outdoors for part of the time provided he is not allowed to run about much (he could be kept in a small run) and is protected from strong sunlight. Ask your veterinary surgeon and be guided by what he says.

If the dog is not allowed out the floor of the room must be protected. If possible, carpets should be removed but if this is impracticable two thick layers of newspapers with a thin sprinkling of sawdust in between is usually sufficient.

Of course a kennel is much more practical, but it should be a large one of the shed type, in which there is room for a table, a good light, and ample space for handling. A cramped kennel in which it is impossible to stand upright is obviously not a suitable sick-room! House dogs will usually be nursed in a spare room, to which reference has already been made.

Whichever is used, good ventilation without a draught must be ensured. Stuffy sick-rooms are an abomination. In winter the temperature should be kept to 16°C (60°F). A room thermometer is useful. Whatever form of heating is arranged, it must be absolutely safe. If it is impossible to arrange this, the dog can be kept perfectly warm with light rugs and hot-water bottles and, if necessary, he can wear a woolly coat. The hot-water bottle should be regularly refilled. If the dog is well enough to be out of his bed most of the time artificial heating will be necessary only in cold weather. Fresh air is essential and provided the dog is warm, and in lung cases wears a pneumonia jacket (see p. 58), he will come to no harm.

Cleanliness of both the patient and his surroundings is essential. The room itself should be kept spotless and any excreta removed immediately. The dog should be groomed daily if well enough, and even if he cannot be moved from his bed it is usually possible to brush him gently with a soft brush or massage his skin with your fingers. If the dog is very ill he must not be disturbed for anything but essentials, but in the ordinary way the average well-cared-for dog, especially in the long-coated breeds, will appreciate this gentle grooming, just as a human patient will feel better for the refreshing daily wash.

The bed should be sufficiently roomy for the dog to turn and stretch in comfort. For small dogs, a tea-chest on its side with a three- to four-inch board nailed across the bottom of the opening, or perhaps a collapsible cage (see page 13), will be found very useful. They keep out draughts and the dog will feel cosy and private. The front can have a wired door if the patient is a restless puppy, running a high temperature, and determined to commit suicide by leaving his box and lying in an icy draught from the room door.

The bedding can be straw, pine-shavings or paper-shavings or blan-

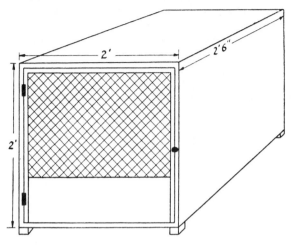

Figure 3

A useful bed for sick puppies. This can be made to any size. The above is suitable for small- and medium-sized breeds. A smaller bed can be placed inside

kets. The latter should be used only for clean cases, and it is a useful idea to have the blankets covered by a small linen sheet or light flannelette cot blanket which can be easily washed and frequently renewed. Nowadays, the modern polyester fur rugs have generally superceded the blanket (*see* Vetbeds page 13).

The tea-chest plan is useful when the dog is suffering from a nervous disease, as it is possible to arrange a sack or blanket to shade the front opening and keep the patient inside sleeping in the dark without having the whole room darkened.

Whatever bedding is used, it must be kept clean and often renewed. If straw is used, shake it up frequently as it can become packed into a hard lump. When changing the bedding of a very sick dog have another box beside you lined with a thick blanket and place him gently in this while you see to his bed.

When a dog is incontinent (this often happens in paralysis) several newspapers arranged under his hindquarters will help to keep the bed dry. Incontinent pads can be bought from large chemists, but, if not, cottonwool arranged between the thighs and under the tail is a great help and a gentle sponging with very weak Dettol and warm water two or three times a day is advisable. Talcum powder used regularly helps to prevent soreness on the abdomen, and zinc ointment should be used for the same purpose in cases of diarrhoea. The dog must not be made wet but he must be kept clean. Long-haired dogs should have the hair cut off round the tail and hindquarters or the tail can be enclosed in a muslin bag which can be burnt when soiled.

Any treatment, simple or complicated, must be carried out with the unhurried speed which characterises the good nurse. To ensure this, have everything ready beforehand. For example, for cleaning the animal you will need cottonwool, lint (for washing), a basin with Dettol and warm water at the correct temperature, a receiver for soiled material, talcum powder, zinc ointment, scissors (for long-haired dogs) and a thick towel to arrange under the hindquarters to keep the bed dry. These articles should be placed on a tray, the home equivalent of the hospital dressing trolley! The window should be shut if any process is likely to chill the patient, and a covered hot-water bottle afterwards is very comforting in cold weather. Handle the dog gently but firmly, supporting him if necessary for feeding and drinking, and be especially gentle in the care of the paralysed patient. (See Paralysis.) Remember that the patient unable to protect himself is easily bruised and injured just in the same way as a dog under anaesthesia. These animals are particularly subject to bed-sores (see p. 68) and must be turned every two hours or so, and their beds kept smooth and soft.

It is important in nursing a sick dog to do what is necessary and no more. In other words, leave the animal to sleep between food and treatment; undisturbed quiet is an essential part of recovery. Of course this does not mean neglect, such as leaving a dog for hours and hours in a wet bed with a cold bottle and a raging thirst. But there is always a great temptation to be over-attentive to the patient, especially if dearly loved, and self-control must be exercised by the nurse. Try to keep calm and cheerful, even if feeling the reverse, as dogs are very sensitive to the tone of voice.

Diet, taking temperatures, post-operative care, and so on, will be found under specific headings.

The pulse is best felt in the femoral artery which crosses the thigh. The normal rate is between seventy and ninety beats per minute, smaller dogs having a faster rate than the bigger breeds.

After feeding, the mouth should be swabbed out with a weak solution of permanganate of potash and water, and this can be repeated every two or three hours during the day if the dog is feverish and thirsty. Sponging the face and head is very refreshing in hot weather and helps to reduce a high temperature. Try to put yourself in the dog's place and foresee and prevent discomfort. To take a tiny example – bright sun shining into the dog's eyes. Understanding, imagination and common sense are all qualities valuable in the canine nurse. Quiet is essential with nerve cases and, indeed, in any serious illness; if you have ever been ill yourself you will remember how irritating you found the banging door, the clattering footsteps and the loud voice.

It is essential to co-operate with your veterinary surgeon. Try to contact him early in the day and not wait until the symptoms become really serious (perhaps late at night) before ringing him. Even when the patient is a pet dog it is useful to keep a daily report for your veterinary surgeon's sake and for your own. Remember, observation is vital for the amateur nurse. In a kennel it is still more important; it is so easy to forget some important symptom when there are a number of patients. So keep a brief daily report, giving temperatures, conditions (for instance, whether having diarrhoea and/or vomiting, discharge of any kind, a cough or showing signs of pain or restlessness), state of the eyes (whether clear or discharging and painful), appetite (good or bad), whether drowsy or alert, and so on. Any new symptom should be noted in detail. Your veterinary surgeon only sees the animal for a short time whereas you may have been with him all day. Details of the treatment given are also useful, not to the veterinary surgeon perhaps, but to the owner. These simple case histories are most useful for future reference.

Try to keep calm and not let your patient see if you are worried as your feelings can easily be picked up by the patient! Sick animals need plenty of rest and sleep, so try to carry out any treatments with the minimum of handling and fuss and have everything ready, so you do not prolong it unnecessarily – a sick dog is easily tired. If you have a bitch due to whelp for the first time, especially if you are inexperienced, or a bitch which has had trouble before, let your veterinary surgeon know the approximate whelping date.

Convalescence should be a leisurely affair, especially in the case of hard-pad and distemper where fits can make their appearance several weeks after the illness. Exercise should be strictly regulated to exclude rushing about or excitement. Diet should be nourishing (*see* post-operative care) and cod liver oil and malt, Collovet (C. Vet) and a suitable vitamin and mineral supplement should all be given to a dog recovering from a serious illness.

Good nursing can make all the difference in illness, and if the nurse needs a reward she can take pleasure in the comments of her friends: 'Nobody would think that dog had been ill so recently – he looks as fit as a fiddle.'

Remember that however clever your veterinary surgeon is, he is terribly handicapped if the dog's owner is careless, forgetful and casual, cannot be bothered to look after the dog properly, and forgets half the advice. He must be able to rely on the conscientious carrying out of his orders and be able to feel that the animal is being given every chance to recover. In the medical profession doctors and surgeons rely on the nursing staff, whether in hospitals or on private cases, to care for the patient properly, and I think they would be the first to admit that their work would be often useless but for this efficient nursing service. Technical training and skill cannot be expected in the majority of home nurses charged with the care of their dogs, but common sense, observation, imagination and kindness are qualities which a veterinary surgeon values greatly, and are not so difficult to acquire.

Veterinary Nursing

Since this book was written, there have been many advances in the field of veterinary surgery and medicine and they have been dealt with by my co-author, Mr Edgson. However, nursing also has altered quite considerably and I would like to give here some of the changes in this field.

When this book was originally written, veterinary nursing had no official recognition. Each veterinary surgeon trained his own assistant, most of whom were extremely competent in every way, but it was a rather 'hit and miss' method. Nowadays veterinary nurses go through a period of training laid down by the Royal College of Veterinary Surgeons which is, in many ways, analogous to that used for human nursing. The RANAS (Registered Animal Nursing Auxiliaries) as they were were first called, are now known as Registered Veterinary Nurses. When the scheme was first evolved, the Royal College of Nursing objected to the word 'nurse' being used for veterinary nurses, but happily the objection seems to have been overcome. The training, which is theoretical and practical, takes place in approved veterinary establishments and two examinations, preliminary and final, are taken. Student nurses wear a green and white striped dress and white apron and qualified nurses a green dress and white apron. So what was once a rather anomalous position has become a highly skilled occupation. All sorts of sophisticated apparatus and treatments are handled, including intravenous techniques much used in cases of shock and the very serious disease parvovirus.

Everything is made as convenient as possible. Injections, for instance – no sterilisation by boiling of metal syringes and needles any more, but a ready sterilised plastic syringe and needle used once and then discarded.

Small animal medicine is now one of the major areas of veterinary surgery instead of being rather the 'Cinderella' side of the profession. Many veterinary surgeons up and down the country concentrate on small animal treatment with modern hospitals and a team of dedicated helpers, including, of course, the nursing staff, at their disposal. This has brought with it the not-so-happy concomitant that animals usually need to be taken to the veterinary surgeon or hospital and house visits are very rare indeed. Sometimes, in small country practices, house visits are still made, but mostly the patient has to travel to the hospital. This is not always a good thing, with a whelping bitch for instance, removed suddenly from her safe familiar surroundings to a clinical environment! In this case, of course, it may be essential, especially if a caesarian section needs to be carried out. It certainly saves time for the veterinary surgeon and he has all equipment to hand, plus a skilled staff to help. Speaking as a breeder, though, it is not always the ideal situation and some animals may be exposed to some stress.

However, many animals are still nursed at home after surgical operations and during illnesses, with the possible exception of parvovirus. As mentioned, treatment for this extremely serious disease can involve intravenous fluid replacement as the animal is often severely dehydrated, and this requires skilled veterinary care and nursing.

Home nursing has not changed that much, but there are one or two modern 'helps' which were not available when this book was first written. One of these is a spray aerosol called Bitter Apple (Groomex) which is excellent to deter a dog from chewing his bandages or plaster. Then there are the excellent polyester fur fabric beds made by various firms. I have found Vetbed to be the best of these. The beds are very soft and warm and are porous, so if you have an incontinent patient, moisture goes straight through to newspapers underneath and the surface stays dry. They are easily washed (use the 'Delicates' washing machine programme) and are excellent for whelping bitches and baby puppies. In fact I use them for my dogs in preference to any other bedding. Another useful item is the collapsible cage sold in varying sizes by kennel manufacturers. With a blanket laid over the top and sides to keep out draughts and give privacy they are very useful for sick dogs. Where these are unsuitable for some reason, artificial barriers can easily be made to prevent the patient walking round unnecessarily.

3

Index to Treatment and Care of Common Troubles

Abdominal Pain

The causes of pain in the abdomen are many and varied. They may be serious or due only to a dietary indiscretion, and are often transitory in nature.

Symptoms will vary slightly according to the gravity of the condition and the location or cause of the pain. However, the following symptoms will be seen to varying degrees according to the severity of the pain.

Restlessness or moving from one spot to another every few minutes. Dogs with gastritis often try to find a cold spot to lie on and rest with their abdomen on, say, a stone floor. Salivation is often present and vomiting is quite usual. If this is recurrent, and it is suspected that a bone or other foreign object has been swallowed, contact your veterinary surgeon immediately. If not, give mixture 1. (See Appendix, p. 84).

Poisons. Certain irritant poisons produce acute abdominal pain (see Poisons), and such cases should be dealt with in the way suggested. If a poison is suspected but its precise nature not known, an emetic (a lump of washing soda pushed down the throat) will empty the stomach of any left there. These cases should receive veterinary attention, as by the time the symptoms of abdominal pain are seen a fair proportion of the agent will have been absorbed from the intestines.

Food poisoning is also dealt with under Poisoning, and this is perhaps the commonest cause of abdominal pain, especially in the young dog or the scavenger type. Dogs with a 'dustbin stomach' often pick up stale or 'high' food, and the resultant diarrhoea and abdominal pain is nature's way of getting rid of it and also teaching the animal a lesson! Unfortunately the lesson does not always work. (See Food Poisoning, p. 60.)

Intestinal colic. The dog may whimper occasionally in cases of indigestion associated with attacks of colicky pain, and gentle massage of the abdomen often relieves these cases. Ordinary bicarbonate of soda (½ teaspoonful–1 dessertspoonful) in milk or water will also greatly assist these cases of mild colic. If the pain is severe, ½–1 teaspoonful of brandy may be added to this mixture. Local warmth, such as a covered hot-water bottle, is important in these cases, and assists in alleviating pain.

Foreign body. If there is any suspicion of the animal having swallowed a foreign body, e.g. stones, sticks, bones, needle, a ball and so on, it is as well not to give anything by mouth until he has been seen by a veterinary surgeon. Above all, do not give a purgative as this will often produce injury to the bowel wall around the foreign object, and, of course, subsequent peritonitis. If a foreign body is really suspected, the least done the better, except for keeping the patient warm and quiet. A *little* brandy, white of egg and water (not giving more than a total of 1 teaspoonful of fluid at any one time) may be given if pain is very severe or if the vomiting is very frequent. (See also Foreign Bodies, p. 36.)

Whelping is a time when abdominal pain is evident. Any cases of straining or of abdominal discomfort about nine weeks after the last show of colour should be regarded as suspicious. Even bitches that are said to have 'never been let out' sometimes produce a litter most unexpectedly! (See also p. 74.)

Constipation. The opposite to enteritis, i.e. constipation, can produce straining with little or no result. In such cases of abdominal pain it is important that the state of constipation is verified, as owners often mis-diagnose this not very common complaint in dogs. Frequent straining can come from diarrhoea, and it would not be the first time that a whelping case was thought to be one of constipation.

Where the cause is definitely attributable to constipation the following is the best course to adopt: Firstly give 1 dessertspoonful–2 tablespoonsful of olive oil or medicinal paraffin according to the size of the dog. Make the diet as fluid, light and laxative as possible by eliminating biscuits, etc., and substituting a little All-Bran. Half the initial dose of oil should be given after the meal, and exercise should be given ½–1 hour after feeding. If no bowel action is seen within 12 hours of the initial dosing a dose of Epsom salts dissolved in a little milk should be given. A dog of 12 kilos (30 lb) should receive a level teaspoonful of the salts, and others according to size. If this has not produced a bowel action within 6–8 hours it is advisable that the animal should be given an enema (see p. 33) or be seen by a veterinary surgeon.

Injury. In cases of abdominal pain associated with a recent injury it is best to have the animal examined by a veterinary surgeon as soon as possible. Above all, give nothing by mouth, especially if there is any vomiting. Such injuries may only be severe bruising of the abdominal muscles; on the other hand, internal damage may be severe and will be aggravated by any food or liquid entering the stomach.

Certain rarer conditions may produce abdominal pain, e.g. intussusception, where the symptoms are similar to those of an intestinal foreign body. This is where a portion of the bowel becomes inverted upon itself. It is commonest in the young dog or puppy. Vomiting is a constant feature, with a temperature rise of 39–40°C (102.5–104°F), and intermittent straining. Diarrhoea is a frequent forerunner of this and such a chain of symptoms in a young dog should be regarded as probably indicative of this state, and your veterinary surgeon informed promptly as the only treatment is surgical. This condition appears to be commonest in the long-backed breeds (e.g. Dachshunds).

Renal pain (i.e. kidney pain) is also a cause of abdominal pain. This may be due to acute nephritis (inflammation of the kidneys) or to renal calculi. Acute nephritis is often due to an infection in young dogs, caused by leptospira canicola.

The symptoms of leptospira canicola infection are those of a severe lumbar pain, with the back arched, a fever of about 40°C (104°F), vomiting, thirst, and refusal to eat. It is essential that treatment is applied immediately. Whilst the infection is present damage is being done to the kidneys, and though delayed treatment will kill the organism, irremediable damage will have been done to the kidneys. Therefore in all cases of this nature your veterinary surgeon must be informed. Incidentally, this particular organism can be quite effectively vaccinated against, in the healthy dog, and if this is done and repeated annually, the animal should be immune for the rest of its life. The vaccination consists of two small injections given at two weeks interval and produces no reaction in the dog. In view of the seriousness of this disease, a policy of prevention is particularly wise where two or more dogs are kept together.

Renal calculi (stones in the kidney), a condition of older dogs, is comparatively rare, and an X-ray examination is necessary to diagnose it. Pain is acute at times and the dog is sometimes unable to move until the spasm passes.

Rubarth's disease (contagious hepatitis) is symptomised in its acute form by severe abdominal pain, vomiting, depression and a temperature of up to 41°C (106°F). In this condition, which is due to a minute virus which attacks the liver, it is important to call in your veterinary surgeon immediately. It is mainly an infection affecting young dogs and it is sometimes noticed within a day or two of a dog having been given a worm dose. A little glucose water is the only medicament that should be given until he has been examined by a veterinary surgeon.

Abortion

Abortion, or miscarriage, is the expulsion of puppies before they have reached their full stage of development in the mother's uterus. The principal difference between abortion and premature whelping is that in the latter the puppies have a good chance of survival if kept very warm, whereas in the former the foeti (as these undeveloped puppies are called) are invariably dead. It is not a very common occurrence, although some bitches show a tendency to abort at about the fifth week of pregnancy, sixty-three days being a normal term.

The causes can be broadly divided into three: disease, endocrine deficiencies and accident. Into the first category come the virus diseases, particularly hard-pad and distemper, which may affect the reproductive organs very considerably; metritis (inflammation of the uterus), probably from an infection acquired at the time of mating, and other serious conditions. The question of endocrine imbalance mentioned in the second category, is a complex subject but which can now be identified and sometimes treated; suffice it to say that for the growth of the embryos in the uterus to be maintained there has to be a proper balance of those hormones particularly affecting fertility in the bitch. The third category – accidents – needs no explanation and includes all hazards from jumping over high fences to being hit by a slammed door. Even upset or change may start a miscarriage in highly strung bitches. A further possible cause, which has yet to be proved with absolute certainty, is an insufficiency of Vitamin E, the so-called fertility vitamin which appears to be necessary to maintain the health and fertility of the reproductive organs.

The symptom of an impending abortion is haemorrhage, usually fairly profuse but sometimes only slight, from the vagina at or about five weeks from the time of mating. Prevention of abortion is not always possible, although avoidance of accidents is, of course, an obvious measure. Bitches in whelp should not be allowed to indulge in riotous games with other dogs; a quiet life with no violent exercise or excitement is essential. Apart from accident, the cause must be found by the veterinary surgeon who must be consulted immediately haemorrhage is noticed. Expert treatment may prevent the threatened

17

abortion, and if a bitch has once aborted without any apparent reason the veterinary surgeon should be consulted before the bitch is again mated. Pending professional treatment, the bitch must be kept absolutely quiet and if necessary given a sedative such as Veganin. (See Appendix, p. 85, for dosage.)

Abscesses

Abscesses are localised centres of infection and are a common sequel to bites and minor skin injuries which have become infected. Whilst injuries of this nature, if treated properly, should not develop into abscesses, bites especially may go unnoticed for several days after they have become infected. The affected area is then hot and painful to the touch, and a lump develops, varying in size according to the injury, the type and degree of infection present. Sometimes the animal will show malaise and a fever as in cases of mastitis (see p. 47), a comparable condition which is really an abscess of a milk gland.

The hair round the lump or swelling should be thoroughly clipped as close to the skin as possible, and then the affected area should be well fomented with warm water, that is, at a temperature in which you can *comfortably* bear your own hand. To this water may be added a little antiseptic such as Dettol, using about 1 teaspoonful of antiseptic to 1 pint of water. A cottonwool pad, soaked in the warm solution, should be held over the area for ½–1 minute, then resoaked and reapplied to the abscess. If the affected area is near the eyes, use warm water only, in order to avoid the risk of the antiseptic running into these delicate organs. The fomenting should be carried out for about 5 minutes (by the clock) and can be repeated as frequently as is possible.

It is wise to inform your veterinary surgeon as soon as the abscess is discovered as lancing may be necessary, or he may advise a course of injections which will quickly dispel the heat and pain and eliminate fever if this is present. Many cases if caught sufficiently early do not need lancing: the antibiotics, e.g. penicillin, in general use being particularly effective against the type of bacteria usually found in these infections.

If the abscess is in an area where a bandage may be easily applied alternative measures may be used. Clip and bathe the surrounding skin as before, then apply some warmed kaolin poultice BP to a bandage (2″ or 3″), fold this over on itself, so that there is always a layer of bandage between the poultice and the animal's skin, then bandage this over the affected area. Be careful not to bandage too tightly. This procedure should be repeated every 6 hours, or until the veterinary surgeon has seen the case. The advantage of a kaolin or antiphlogistine poultice is that the kaolin will continue to 'draw' the infection all the time it is on the skin, whereas an ordinary fomentation with warm water must be repeated frequently in order to be really beneficial. (See also Appendix, p. 85.)

If the abscess has burst spontaneously, thoroughly wash and cleanse the skin wound and the abscess cavity two or three times daily until healing has taken place. For this an antiseptic solution as above may be used. A gentle squeezing towards the point of rupture of the abscess will ensure the evacuation of all accumulated pus and discharge, and hasten the healing process.

The cavity should be kept clean and not be allowed to close until healing takes place from within.

Accidents

Street accidents can be divided into two main groups:

1. Superficial injuries (varying degrees of bruising, skin lacerations and possibly minor bone fracture.
2. Severe injury (fractures, profuse haemorrhages, possibility of damage to internal organs).

Superficial Injury

The patient is usually more frightened than hurt and is generally more difficult to handle than the badly injured dog. Restraint is the most important factor; a semi-hysterical dog in a crowd is not only distressing but also dangerous. If possible, handling should be left to the owner, whom the dog will usually trust. A lead slipped over the dog's head as a noose is a useful method of catching an hysterical animal. A few minutes spent soothing the animal before endeavouring to see the extent of the injuries are not wasted; he will be given a chance to get over the initial shock and surprise of the accident. (See p. 6.)

Remove him to a quiet spot as soon as possible and, if he can walk or be carried, take him indoors. If the injuries seem to be confined to the extremities, and there is no sign of bleeding from nose or mouth, a sedative should be given if the dog is still excited. Attention may then be paid to his injuries. A dog capable of getting up and running off after an accident is usually only slightly injured.

For wounds see p. 77. Fractures, p. 39.

Any wounds should be gently bathed and a clean handkerchief or bandage applied to wounds on extremities.

Severe Injury

The animal may be unconscious or unable to rise. Do not try to lift him as this may cause pain and he may snap or bite unintentionally. In addition, further damage may be done. Get a sack, blanket or coat, lay it on the ground and gently and gradually slide it under him. Then, using this as a stretcher, carry him into a quiet spot or room, or place him on the back seat of a car. Profuse haemorrhage should be stopped or stemmed. This can best be done in an emergency by wedging a handkerchief, the cleaner the better, into the wound. If on a limb, a handkerchief tied round the wound will help. If there is no external sign of injury, but haemorrhage is seen from the nose or mouth, keep the animal as quiet as possible until help arrives, or until he is taken to the veterinary surgeon. Keep the animal as still and as warm as circumstances permit. Cover him with a blanket, rug or coat and, if possible, place a hot-water bottle along his spine. (See also Haemorrhage, p. 41.)

If there is any suspicion of internal injury, or if there is any blood round the mouth or nose, or if the animal is unconscious, do not give any stimulant or sedative. With a severely injured dog the best action is to check local haemorrhages and keep the patient warm and quiet until skilled help is obtained.

Artificial Respiration

The object of artificial respiration is to provide the animal with sufficient air (oxygen) when respiratory failure (i.e., stoppage of natural breathing) has occurred. Respiratory collapse, or failure, is found mainly during surgery, when an animal is anaesthetised, but poisoning by narcotics, coal gas or smoke may produce this state.

Action must of course be prompt as, if the heart is still functioning but respiration has ceased, it is a matter of minutes before the animal suffocates. If there is no heart action discernible the animal is almost certainly already dead, but artificial respiration should always be tried where there is any hope.

Procedure

Put the animal on a table, its left side uppermost and with the head hanging down over the edge, open the mouth and pull the tongue well out, if possible having an assistant to keep the mouth open and the tongue out during the attempts to restart respiration. If no assistance is to hand, a roll of bandage, a cotton reel or similar object may be used to wedge the mouth open. Always make sure there is no mucus in the throat, by wiping the back with a handkerchief or cottonwool. Grasp the left foreleg firmly just above the elbow (i.e. where the leg is attached to the body) and with the leg grasped in the hand, 'pump' downwards and slightly towards the back end of the dog. This should be done firmly, and then the pressure released. The action should be repeated every 5 seconds. This has the effect of compressing the chest cavity when the ribs are pressed by the fist, and then the natural elasticity of the tissues will result in their expansion when the pressure is temporarily removed.

If respirations begin, a bottle of smelling-salts held underneath the head will rapidly improve their strength and regularity. A few drops of neat brandy on the back of the throat are useful as an additional stimulant.

Asthma (symptoms of). See Heart Attacks (p. 42).

Bites

Dogs are most commonly bitten by another dog, a cat or a rat. For Snake Bites see p. 67.

Dog Bites
There is invariably some degree of penetration with this injury, and it is important that a close watch be kept on such injuries until they have completely healed, as abscess formation is a constant danger if healing of the skin wound is too rapid. Immediately the bite is found the hair should be clipped away from the wound. This is very necessary with the long-haired breeds. A thorough search should be made for other wounds; these often have only small skin openings and may be easily overlooked. The wounds should then be thoroughly cleansed with cottonwool soaked in warm water containing a suitable antiseptic.

Any injury near the eyes should be swabbed with warm water *only*. This should be done twice daily for at least 5 days, and in the event of any heat or hardness developing in the injured region a veterinary surgeon should be informed.

If larger than about half an inch, any tear in the skin alone, or skin and muscle, should be seen at once by a veterinary surgeon in order that any stitching that may be necessary can be carried out promptly. It is important that such wounds are not left many hours as once secondary infection occurs and granulation tissue form, a wound cannot be stitched satisfactorily.

21

Bites on the head, limbs or genitalia should be regarded with especial caution, and veterinary advice sought if in doubt. Bites by dogs with powerful jaws may result in fracture, or puncture, of a bone or a joint, and such wounds can only be satisfactorily treated systemically, as well as locally, by a veterinary surgeon. Small centres of infection are left embedded deeply in the tissue, and these centres may form abscesses at a later stage, unless a course of antibiotics is given to prevent this. (Abscesses, see p. 18.)

Cat Bites

Cat bites, fortunately, are not very common in dogs as cats generally prefer to scratch and run. However, when they do occur they should be thoroughly cleansed, hair being clipped away from the points of entry, and then swabbed. Usually it is advisable to have the animal injected with penicillin or some other anti-infective agent. Cat bites are notoriously dirty, and the wound is of the puncture variety, i.e. deep, with a small point of entry, and therefore provides inadequate drainage. This is true also of:

Rat Bites

Here again local treatment should be carried out, but systemic treatment is more or less essential to avoid complications. Rats carry an infection called leptospiral jaundice, which can easily be fatal to dogs who have no protection against the disease. It is wise, therefore, following a local dressing and cleansing of the wound (which the owner can usually do quite satisfactorily) to have the animal given a dose of antiserum, and/or suitable antibiotic. This will prevent the much more dangerous complication of leptospiral infection. All dogs should be immunised against this disease, especially if they are employed as ratters or farm dogs and are likely to be in contact in any way with these vermin.

Details of vaccination:

Vaccination against leptospira icterrohaemorrhagia infection is a simple process, which is carried out in the healthy dog and which will protect him for the rest of his life. The vaccination consists of two small injections, 1 or 2 ml only, given subcutaneously at an interval of two weeks. There are no ill effects after these injections and the dog will be immune to the disease within a few days of the second injection. It is important to boost the immunity each year, and this is usually done by using one of the combined vaccines covering other diseases as well.

Brain, Inflammation of

Under this general heading can be grouped encephalitis, meningitis, the involvement of the brain during uraemia and advanced kidney diseases, acute toxaemia, and so on.

The symptoms may come suddenly as with a fit, or may appear gradually. Although the animal seems conscious he is, for the most part, more or less oblivious of his surroundings although there may be occasional periods of comparative lucidity. He does not recognise his owners, although he will react to food and sometimes to loud noises. In mild cases the dog tends to wander about aimlessly and restlessly with a vacant expression; in more serious cases he will walk round in small circles, always in the same direction and, if restrained, will struggle to continue this circling. Violent cases will try to climb the wall and bump into obstacles. Often the dog will cry, whine or howl, and the high-pitched typical meningeal yelp is a very distressing and ominous symptom.

Pending a veterinary examination, the dog should be given a suit-able sedative or tranquilliser and put in a darkened, empty room or a large kennel where he cannot injure himself, until professional help has been consulted. Ice packs or cloths wrung out in very cold water are often useful when applied to the back of the skull during a quiet period.

Except in very mild cases the prognosis of this condition is guarded, and where permanent damage to the brain exists recovery is unlikely; it may be kinder to have the animal put to sleep. The veterinary surgeon should be asked his frank opinion of the dog's chances. He should always be consulted immediately whenever the brain is involved.

If treatment is to be tried, such as general anaesthesia for some hours to rest the brain or powerful sedatives, the sooner it is begun the better. As it can be provided only by a qualified person, one should be consulted without delay.

Bruising

Bruises come from a variety of causes, but doubtless the commonest is an argument between dog and automobile. Whilst bruising is not likely to produce more than a temporary stiffness in a young dog, in old ones neglected bruising may leave a chronic myositis (a type of rheumatism). In addition, with severe cases of bruising in old dogs, the histamine-like products released from the damaged tissues may produce kidney embarrassment and some degree of shock.

The injured area should first be searched for any minor cuts or grazes. These should be bathed and cleansed with a little warm antiseptic solution. Warm compresses to the bruised area will greatly relieve the local pain. A hot-water bottle, a warmed pad of Thermogene wool or a kaolin poultice BP provide the local heat required. A little warm water by mouth with glucose added is advisable as a mild stimulant, and if the bruising is extensive, and as a routine with old dogs, it is wise to give a little bicarbonate of soda or milk of magnesia every two or three hours until about twelve hours after the injury. This by its alkalising action helps to counteract any acidosis or kidney impairment. According to the size of the dog, ½–1 teaspoonful is adequate, and this amount can quite easily be given dissolved in a little warm water or warm milk.

Limited exercise should be given for 5–7 days following the injury, and diet should be light and preferably fluid. Particularly for old dogs, where the bruising may have been extensive, barley water for a week or so is better than ordinary drinking water.

Burns and Scalds

A burn is an injury produced by dry heat and a scald by moist heat, but the first-aid treatment is the same for both. Except in very minor cases, these injuries need immediate treatment by a veterinary surgeon. Shock is present in all moderately or seriously burnt or scalded dogs and the prognosis for the latter, if extensive, is not good. Toxaemia and sepsis are common secondary consequences.

The dog should be treated for shock (see p. 67) and placed in a bed, lightly but warmly covered and made as comfortable as possible. A teaspoonful of bicarbonate of soda should be given by mouth and the dog should be encouraged to drink warm milk with glucose, as fluid is most important in injuries of this kind. The burn or scald should receive emergency treatment as follows: the hair over and surrounding the area should be removed with round-topped surgical scissors and the wound covered with dry bicarbonate of soda applied thickly, or with a pad soaked in a solution of bicarbonate of soda and water, one ounce to one pint of boiled water. Infection of such injuries is common, so everything used should be scrupulously clean and the wound covered as quickly as possible. On no account should grease, oil or ointment be used. Very small burns can be successfully treated with an anti-inflammatory preparation, or similar bland ointment.

The diet of burnt or scalded dogs should in due course be especially rich in the protein (body-building) foods such as meat, and extra supplies should be given to help in the repair of the injured tissues. The extra protein is equally necessary in accident cases and wherever there is serious injury, as soon as a normal diet is allowed.

Choking

This is fortunately not very common, but that it is a very dangerous and urgent condition requiring immediate attention will be appreciated when it is realised that death from asphyxiation can take place within two minutes. The reader is advised to make himself completely familiar with the procedure outlined below – if choking actually occurs there will be no time to refer to books.

Some dogs have smaller gullets than others and are even unable to swallow quite small pieces of meat without choking. Meat should be given in really tiny bits or in large chunks impossible to swallow whole. Sometimes two pieces are joined together by gristle and this often causes choking.

Be careful what you give to dogs for playthings. Rubber toys are particularly dangerous; they can be fatal if wedged in the throat.

The symptoms of choking are alarming; sometimes the dog makes little noise but falls over on his side and shows every sign of asphyxiation, with cyanosed tongue, and so on. Left untreated, he will die in a few moments. You must prise open the dog's jaws – sometimes considerable force is necessary – by pressing on the back molars and pressing down the lower jaw with the other hand. Then, holding the mouth open as wide as possible, you must try either to hook up the offending object with your forefinger or, if this is impossible, push it down. Often the dog will vomit in the latter case and rid himself of the meat, or whatever it is. You must be prepared to be bitten in a good cause as the dog will be frantic with fear and will not know what he is doing, but if you work at top speed, efficiently and decisively, you will probably be successful. If a friend is present who can hold the dog's jaws open while you remove the obstruction so much the better, but it is usually an emergency to be tackled single-handed. This is a matter where only the dog owner can save his animal's life – even if the veterinary surgeon lived next door it would be too late to call him – you must act immediately and at top speed, as only heroic measures are likely to be successful.

With bones, the need is not as a rule so urgent and although the dog will make definite choking noises, paw at his mouth and be acutely uncomfortable, there is not usually much danger from asphyxiation. Once again the mouth should be opened and the bone should be removed if feasible, as gently as possible as the throat is easily lacerated. If it seems firmly wedged use no force but try to loosen it with your finger, but if it seems fixed it becomes a matter for a veterinary surgeon. Usually these cases call mainly for knack, but as pain and injury are so easily caused by clumsy handling it is always wise to call in professional assistance where difficulty is experienced.

To sum up, be careful what you give your dog (there is no point in running unnecessary risks) and if choking occurs drop everything and act AT ONCE.

Collapse

This serious condition resembles shock but is very much more severe and often has a fatal outcome. It may come as the result of a bad accident, in heart conditions (see p. 42) or as a disquieting phenomenon in a serious disease, and recovery will depend on cause.

The dog should be treated for shock (see p. 67); in addition, the hindquarters should be raised and the head kept low. The dog should be on its right side. Brandy by mouth (a few drops on the back of the tongue) should be given if the animal is able to swallow – nothing should ever be given by mouth to an unconscious patient. If the dog is unconscious the tongue should be pulled forward and out; if it falls to the back of the throat it will impede respiration. Transfusion and heart stimulants may be given, but these are for the veterinary surgeon to decide, and in all cases of collapse one should be consulted at once.

Concussion

This is due to accidents, blows on the head and similar causes. The dog is usually unconscious for most of the time, and the veterinary surgeon should be contacted at once. In the meantime, place the animal, well covered with blankets, somewhere warm and quiet. Hotwater bottles are advisable but they must be properly covered as an unconscious and possibly restless patient is easily burnt. If possible, ice (wrapped in a flannel) should be applied to the head, or cloths wrung out in very cold water and changed repeatedly. Nothing should be given by mouth, and the dog should be kept as quiet as possible pending professional assistance.

Diarrhoea, How to Prevent and Treat

Diarrhoea, the frequent passage of watery motions, is a symptom and not a disease in itself, and, if possible, the cause should be tackled first. In certain illnesses (such as hard-pad) diarrhoea is simply part of the pattern of disease and, as such, is treated specifically but it is often due to other causes – food, worms, indifferent hygiene, for example. Although dogs can eat putrid meat with apparent equanimity, and suffer no obvious harm, its ingestion will often cause diarrhoea. This applies equally to cheap and inferior biscuit meals, some brands of dried meat, stale biscuit, bad fish and poor and tainted food generally.

Diarrhoea in puppies is, unfortunately, a common occurrence in many kennels, but any owner who regards it as normal and of no significance is wrong. A properly reared puppy may have occasional looseness but it should *not* have diarrhoea. When it exists, in spite of first-class conditions and care, the cause may be bacterial and can be remedied by giving certain drugs acting in the intestines. Food for puppies should always be fresh and of excellent quality – no contaminated meat, for instance. The youngsters should not be fed on or near sawdust or straw as if these substances get into food they are frequent causes of diarrhoea. Do not give large, sloppy meals. Diet for puppies is a big subject and is fully dealt with in *The Popular Guide to Puppy-Rearing.*[1] Sudden change to a different kind of food can cause diarrhoea and this often happens at weaning time, when the change from the mother's milk to other foods is made too quickly. Worms are another cause, particularly when the puppy looks emaciated in spite of plenty of food. The diarrhoea is usually frothy when these internal parasites are responsible.

Puppy kennels should be kept scrupulously clean and excreta removed at once if possible. Overcrowding, stuffy conditions, lack of exercise and fresh air can predispose to diarrhoea.

Leaving on one side disease and harmful bacteria as possible reasons, the owner should ask himself just why his dogs or puppies have diarrhoea, and not regard it as a perfectly normal happening.

Although referring mainly to puppies, these remarks are equally applicable to adults.

Diarrhoea occasionally results from mental upsets – for instance, when a dog has been on a long journey for the first time – but these cases are very transitory.

Sometimes diarrhoea assumes an epidemic character and all or

[1]Popular Dogs Publishing Co. Ltd.

most of a kennel may be affected. This may be due to outside causes – for example, bad meat eaten by all the dogs – but in other cases it is a matter for the veterinary surgeon, who should always be consulted when the diarrhoea is not due to any ascertainable cause. It is advisable to take the temperature of an affected dog or puppy, particularly when there is also depression or other signs of malaise. There is usually a slight rise when an infection is the cause.

Prevention of this troublesome condition is, as we have seen, of prime importance and 75 per cent of the cases seen in kennels would be unnecessary with proper care and feeding and good management and hygiene.

Treatment will, of course, depend on the cause. When it is tainted food, a dose of castor oil is a safe preliminary and this may be sufficient to cure a mild case. Otherwise, a careful diet should be started, consisting mainly of milk thickened with arrowroot (see Appendix, p. 84) or cornflour and rice with milk. Do not give meat, fish, eggs, biscuits or glucose. Do not experiment with invalid foods which might aggravate the trouble, and remember that brown bread and wholemeal generally, is relaxing, so better avoided. When the animal is definitely ill, and there is weakness and prostration, Brand's Essence is excellent.

Drugs are not usually necessary in mild, uncomplicated cases, although kaolin and charcoal is a useful standby, and Collis Brown's mixture is often successful in obstinate cases, but as this drug can be very dangerous in amateur hands it should be given only with veterinary approval. As previously mentioned, when the diarrhoea is bacterial in origin there are specific drugs obtainable from the veterinary surgeon, or on prescription, which act directly in the intestines. Do not be persuaded by a chemist into giving patent medicines or proprietary diarrhoea powders of any kind.

Continue with the diet advised for two or three days at least, longer if necessary. Never be in a hurry to return to solid fare; the intestines must have a chance to recover and resume their normal tone by a bland, soothing diet. Make the return to a normal diet in a gradual way via baked custards, white fish boiled in milk, etc., and if there is any diarrhoea go back to the strict diet immediately. Even when ordinary fare is resumed be very careful; the sudden inclusion of rich and unsuitable items, such as herrings, can renew the whole trouble.

Many cases of diarrhoea do not need such an elaborate and strict diet, and if fish is given instead of meat, and two or three additional meals of arrowroot and milk are given, a mild case will make a speedy and complete recovery.

Dislocations

Dislocations occur occasionally in dogs, usually as a result of a car accident. The commonest joint to become dislocated is the hip joint, although in the sporting breeds, especially greyhounds, dislocation of a toe joint is not unusual.

It is generally necessary to have an X-ray examination to verify that there is a dislocation, and that there is no fracture as well. Replacement of the dislocated joint should be done by a veterinary surgeon as soon as possible after the injury, otherwise the blood clot which forms in the injured joint becomes firm, and the dislocated bone difficult to replace. This procedure is usually carried out under a general anaesthetic, so do not feed.

First-aid measures should be confined to keeping the injured limb, which the animal will 'carry', in as near a natural position as possible. With nervous dogs, a sedative (see Appendix, p. 85) can be given, and if this has been done inform the veterinary surgeon who attends the animal.

See also Fractures, p. 39.

Distemper. See Hysteria (p. 44), Nasal Discharge (p. 50).

Dosing

Liquids can be given in a spoon or, if the amount is large, in a small bottle. Always read the instructions on the label and check the dose before giving the medicine. If the dog is a small one, either put him on a table or, if amenable, seat him beside you. Do not attempt to open his jaws but draw the loose skin of the cheek furthest from you outwards to form a pouch, insert the spoon, and slowly pour in the medicine. Withdraw the spoon and your fingers and hold the dog's head up, when he will promptly swallow. With practice, this becomes so easy that a dog can be dosed standing on the ground. A big dog may have to be held between your knees, but he is dosed in the same way. All this may sound difficult but actually it is exceedingly simple, and there should be no ignominious struggle to force medicine down a dog's throat. If you forced his jaws apart and poured the liquid down by thrusting the spoon between his teeth, he would choke and cough and splutter, and what should have been a simple operation would have become an uncomfortable one for both of you. When the medicine is in the form of a pill or tablet it can either be given hidden between two pieces of meat or bread and butter (an 'un-doped' portion should be given before and after the one concealing the pill) or placed right at the back of the tongue. To do this, open the dog's mouth by pressing firmly with finger and thumb on the cheeks between the molar teeth, put the pill in, pushing it with the forefinger well to the back of the tongue. Close the dog's mouth and gently stroke the throat downwards until he swallows. When you are sure the pill has gone, release the dog. Powders can be given in the same way, or they can be mixed with a little milk and given as a liquid. Oily liquids can be given floating on milk; if given by a spoon it should be warmed first. Tasteless medicines may be taken voluntarily when mixed with milk.

See also Appendix, p. 85.

Dysentery

This means blood in the faeces, the motions being watery but containing blood also. All such cases should be seen by a veterinary surgeon, but as a safe first measure arrowroot gruel may be given by mouth *ad lib*. (See Appendix, p. 84.)

Ears

Mishaps to these parts of the dog's anatomy are fairly frequent. The three main causes of trouble are:

1. Torn ears (from fighting or by barbed wire).
2. Haematoma (a haemorrhage under the skin of the ear flap).
3. Foreign bodies in the outer ear canal (e.g. grass seeds).

Torn Ears

If an ear is damaged in a fight, or by sharp wire, it will bleed fairly profusely. In addition, the irritation caused often makes the animal shake his head violently, which adds to the bleeding and also spatters blood in all directions. Blood is a good example of a little going a long way; within a few moments of the injury the dog appears to have lost at least half its total amount. Dogs do not, however, bleed to death from bitten ears, and the bleeding will cease within a few minutes if pieces of cottonwool soaked in cold water are held firmly over the wounded area, one each side of the injured flap. If the wound is extensive, i.e. more than ½" long, it is advisable to have the injury attended by a veterinary surgeon, but before taking him to the surgery bandage the ear upwards over the head, the bandage going right round the neck and thus enveloping the whole ear and neck region. This will stop the dog shaking his head during the journey and so starting a fresh flow of blood. If the wound is small, clean it with a little cold water containing a suitable antiseptic, and with a pad of cottonwool or gauze each side of the ear flap, bandage the ear over the head as described. This may be removed one or two days later, and the wound kept clean until it has healed. In spaniels, and long-coated dogs, it will be necessary to clip some of the hair away to ensure a clean wound.

Haematoma

A dog's ear consists in section of a layer of skin, then a thin layer of cartilage, then a further layer of skin. Occasionally, especially in large-eared dogs, a violent shaking of the head causes a rupture of one of the many small blood vessels supplying the skin and the tissues below. This results in the ear flap becoming suddenly hard and balloon-like. The condition is not serious but may need surgical measures to return the ear to normal size. This, of course, will have to be carried out by a veterinary surgeon. As this condition is usually the result of violent head shaking or ear scratching it is as well to have the ears examined to make sure there is nothing producing an irritation in the ear canal itself. Such an irritation can result from a local infection, or can be produced by:

Foreign Bodies in the Ear

Grass seeds occasionally work their way down the ear, into the external canal of this organ, resulting in an acute irritation. The animal holds its head on one side, whimpers, and is in obvious discomfort. It should be promptly seen by a veterinary surgeon who, by means of an auroscope, will be able to see the seed, and with special forceps remove it. Most cases will require an anaesthetic. The earlier this is attended to the better, as the presence of the grass seed will result in a sore ear, and maybe in secondary infections.

Do *not* pour oil or any other liquid into the ear. This will make the veterinary surgeon's job more difficult, by obscuring his range of vision when he examines the ear with the auroscope.

Do *not* probe or poke about in the ear with forceps or pieces of cottonwool. This will push the grass seed further down and make its removal much more difficult.

Eclampsia

Eclampsia is a condition seen in the bitch and it generally occurs about the time of whelping, or it may occur during the suckling period.

This condition is caused by a lowering of the *blood* calcium which in turn is due to the heavy demands made by various detoxication processes which go on about the time of parturition, and also to the heavy draw on the bitch's reserves by having to produce large amounts of milk. The bitch with a first litter is not commonly affected, it being a condition more usual with the mature mother. Eclampsia is commonest in the bitch with the large litter, especially when she has 'done the puppies well'.

The first symptom is an alteration in temperament. The bitch appears distressed and fussed for apparently no reason. Some bitches become very excited and may even have hysteria. They then become lethargic, have a sub-normal temperature, may show epileptiform convulsions and, in very advanced cases, become cold, comatose and moribund. Any panting, shivering, or unusual distress in an in-milk or lactating bitch should be regarded as possible eclampsia.

The only specific treatment for this deficiency condition is the replacement of the lacking blood calcium. This can be done adequately only by the administration of calcium by injection, and if the condition is suspected your veterinary surgeon should be informed immediately. There is a degree of urgency in these cases as some bitches rapidly become comatose. There are several steps which, if taken promptly, will greatly retard the onset of the advanced symptoms of the condition. Firstly, remove the puppies or allow them to remain in the bitch's presence but do not allow them to feed from her. This will prevent any further immediate drain on her calcium reserves. If the bitch has symptoms of hysteria or over-excitability give a small dose of sedative (2–5 gr. pot. bromide). In any case, keep her absolutely still and quiet and as warm as possible. If available, one or two 5 gr. calcium lactate tablets crushed in a little milk may be given by mouth. These should be continued daily after she has received her calcium injection and until the puppies have been weaned. An adequate supply of Vitamin D should also be given during convalescence.

Prevention of Eclampsia

As this condition is due to a deficiency of calcium in the bloodstream of the nursing bitch much can be done to make its onset less likely by the inclusion of calcium, phosphorus, and so on, in the diet. Bitches should be given both milk and vitamin and calcium supplements such as Stress from the sixth week of pregnancy until the puppies are weaned. Milk is a rich natural source of calcium, and Stress supplies the essential minerals in an easily assimilated form. A rich source of

Vitamin D should always be given as this aids the utilisation of calcium and phosphorus – halibut oil (C. Vet) is a good example.

Enema

An enema is not often needed but is sometimes used in constipation and in illnesses where it is inadvisable to give an aperient or purgative by mouth.

An enema consists of an injection of fluid into the bowel, by means of a syringe. For small dogs a straight glass syringe can be used, but for general use the ordinary Higginson's type of rubber apparatus is preferable. For simple constipation only a small injection is needed – for a toy, half a teaspoonful of glycerine mixed with two tablespoonsful of warm water. For medium-sized dogs double the quantity, and for collie size four times. Soapy water (made from pure soap flakes or Castile soap) can be used instead of glycerine. In the case of a real obstruction – that is, not simple constipation – double the quantity can be given and the enema repeated three or four times.

To give an enema, place the dog on a table – with large dogs, preferably in a yard – and have a jug containing the fluid at a higher level. Fill the syringe, making sure it is full as an injection of air can be very painful. Vaseline the bone point and insert into the rectum for its whole length (about seven inches). Give the injection slowly, then remove the syringe with a quick, smooth movement. Press the dog's flanks together for a few moments to give the enema a chance to act.

After use, wash the syringe in warm, soapy water, rinse in a solution of Dettol and water and hang in a cool place to dry.

A disposable micro-enema is now available and is quite useful (Micralax – Smith Kline).

Eyes

    1. Scratches of the eye.
    2. Foreign bodies.
    3. Extrusion of the eye-ball.

Eyes are extraordinarily delicate and tender organs. Any injury or mishap to them should be examined promptly by a veterinary surgeon. Until this can be done, several measures to increase the chances of full recovery without impairment of vision can be taken.

Scratches from Cats or Thorns

These are the commonest form of injury. The main danger with these scratches is that secondary infection will subsequently occur, resulting in an ulceration of the clear wall of the eye-ball, known as the cornea. Today, penicillin is often used to prevent this, and your veterinary surgeon will be able to advise whether this should or should not be used. The best course for the owner when the injury is found, is to bathe the eye gently with boiled water at about blood heat, using a little cottonwool. Do not try to wipe the actual surface of the eye with wool, but swamp or flush the eye-ball with the water. This eye bath may have added to it a little boracic powder, about 1 saltspoonful to ¼ pint of water. Do *not* use any antiseptic or disinfectant for any eye dressing.

After bathing gently, wipe the surrounding hair and eyelids dry with a little clean cottonwool. Then a few drops of warmed *castor* oil should be dropped or poured into the eye. This oil will have a soothing action and will protect by a thin film the delicate surface of the eye. Pure castor oil should be used, not a substitute.

Foreign Bodies in Eyes

These are comparatively rare in dogs but when they do occur can cause acute irritation.

Sometimes a dog gets a fragment of straw or sawdust in his eye, and in the summer grass seeds and barley haws can cause very serious trouble. Their possible presence is indicated by the dog having one or both eyes tightly shut. There is a profuse watery discharge. Sometimes the lids are swollen, and the dog will rub and paw at its eye.

The eyelids must be separated and the surface carefully examined, the eyelids being turned back gently. Often the foreign body is quite obvious and is readily removable by forceps used with the very greatest care, but sometimes nothing can be seen. If it is impossible to detect the cause of the trouble veterinary advice must be sought at once. When the foreign body appears to be closely adherent to the corneal surface no attempt should be made to remove it with forceps, although a few drops of warm castor oil will sometimes loosen it effectively. Eye lotions should not be used as these may wash the foreign body further in. If castor oil is unsuccessful, veterinary assistance should be obtained as neglect can result in permanent damage to the eye.

Extrusion of the Eye-ball

This condition is confined to the exophthalmic type of dog i.e. those with prominent eyes, such as Pekingese, King Charles Spaniels, etc.

34

In such breeds the condition is not at all rare. The more rapidly the case can be seen and treated by a veterinary surgeon, the better. Delay results in a swelling of the eye-ball itself and of the tissues of the orbital cavity, resulting in the eye-ball tending to protrude again if replaced. Delay can make replacement impossible. If this should become the case total surgical removal of the eye is the only course.

A few minutes spent protecting the eye from damage, however, is not time wasted; indeed, in some cases it is essential. Castor oil should be used liberally, moistening the whole of the eye with it. This helps to keep the eye-ball moist and supple. A pad of cottonwool or gauze soaked in the oil may be gently placed over the eye while the animal is being taken to the surgery. Remember that the eye-ball is very prone to bruising and injury; therefore always use great gentleness.

Summary

1. Always treat cases of eye injury with great care.
2. Avoid touching the eye-ball at all when bathing i.e. flush rather than wipe.
3. Never use antiseptics in or near the eyes.
4. Boiled water cooled to blood heat is the safest eye-wash.
5. Pure castor oil is undoubtedly the most useful first-aid dressing.

Fevers, Feeding in

'Feeding' is a misnomer here as one of the most important points to remember when considering the diet of a sick dog is that an animal with a temperature of over 39.5°C (103°F) should not be fed with normal solid food. The less work the digestive organs have to do, the better, and the lack of appetite usually present is nature's way of pointing out that food is not required as long as fever is present. In fact, excessive feeding can prolong the illness and increase its severity. Fluids are absolutely essential, however, and if the dog will not take them voluntarily they must be given frequently like medicine, a tablespoonful or so at a time. Glucose[1] and boiled water is excellent for this purpose, but not milk as this, although a liquid, is definitely a food. When the temperature has returned to normal a very light fluid diet can be begun, such as milk, beaten-up egg in milk, etc., but any rise in tem-

---

[1] Honey is also excellent – one teaspoonful to a cup of boiled water.

perature should be a signal for a return to glucose and water. Nervous complications in the virus diseases such as hard-pad are far less likely if this method is adopted, and the animal will recover more quickly as he is not being called upon to deal with quantities of food when unable to profit from them. The fluid intake will help very considerably in elimination of water products – always very important in feverish illnesses.

See also Temperature (p. 70).

Fights – Separating Fighting Dogs

Occasionally one has the misfortune to have one's dog attacked by (or even for it to attack!) another dog. Usually, a few well-chosen words, and a sharp tap on the rump with the lead or stick, will divert the aggressor's attention. However, when animals really start fighting it is not a simple matter to stop them. Do not try to separate them with your hands if a stick or lead is available. A walking-stick is ideal; the handle placed through the collar of the attacker and then twisted so that the collar tightens on the throat will make him release his grip, and when separated he is still well under control. A lead, used as a noose, can also be used for this but is not so effective.

Douching with cold water is also a fairly effective method of *temporarily* separating fighting animals, although it is not always possible to have a supply of cold water to hand!

When one dog has a firm, vice-like hold on another, a stick or firm twig pushed between his jaws will quickly make him relax his hold sufficiently to pull the attacked one away. A sharp rap on the tip of the nose is also very effective.

It is as well to remember that the owner of a dog who attacks other dogs is responsible for keeping his dog under proper control, and if your dog is aggressive always keep him on a lead when there are other animals about.

For Bites, Dog (see p. 21).

Fits. See Rabies (p. 66).

Foreign Bodies

Objects which become lodged in various parts of an animal's digestive tract are referred to collectively as foreign bodies. The subject is complex as the object may become arrested at any one of a number of sites. Not only will the symptoms vary but also the seriousness of the situation. Therefore the subject will be discussed from beginning to end, dividing the various types of foreign body cases into geographical or anatomical areas.

1. Mouth.
2. Throat.
3. Gullet (oesophagus).
4. Stomach.
5. Intestines.
6. Rectum.

Mouth

A common form of this mishap is a bit of bone or wood becoming firmly lodged across the roof of the mouth, between the back molars on each side of the upper jaw. Such an object may become tightly fixed. In most instances these can be successfully dislodged by opening the dog's mouth and levering the wedged object out with a finger or the handle end of a spoon. Care should be taken not to allow the dog to close his mouth until the object is well outside the mouth, otherwise he may swallow it. In some cases, however, the object becomes so firmly fixed that dental forceps may be required to dislodge it.

The signs of a foreign body in the mouth are usually obvious. The animal claws and paws frantically at his mouth, salivates profusely, and is, of course, unable to eat food. Whilst such cases are not really dangerous to the animal's life, the sooner the offending object is removed, the better. Needles are a different matter; they may break in the mouth, leaving the point firmly embedded in the palate or tongue. Anaesthesia and an X-ray examination are essential in most of these cases, firstly in order to facilitate the removal of the embedded portion, and secondly to find out whether the broken-off portion has been expelled, or swallowed to cause further trouble lower down.

Throat. See Choking (p. 25).

Gullet (Oesophagus)

It is usually medium-sized portions of bone that become lodged in the oesophagus, the channel which connects the mouth with the stomach. A simple way to identify this condition is to give the animal one or two *small* pieces of meat. If the foreign body is present in the oesophagus the dog will vomit the meat, almost at once. The oesophagus is divided into two main regions – the head or front end situated in the neck region, and the stomach or lower end situated within the chest cavity or thorax. The latter position is a more serious site of obstruc-

37

tion as injury to the gullet in this region endangers many vital organs and nerves. In any case, or suspected case, of oesophageal obstruction X-ray or surgical measures are essential as rapidly as possible, in order to locate and remove the object. Objects in the oesophagus are often spiky or pointed, or have sharp protrusions, and massage of the dog's neck in an endeavour to move the obstruction should be avoided; it might result in laceration of the lining of the gullet.

Stomach

Large, smooth foreign bodies such as golf balls, stones, marbles and bones are the commonest foreign bodies to become arrested in the stomach. The dog may show various signs of distress, according to the amount of inflammation or obstruction. In the stomach, these foreign bodies produce a mechanical gastritis, even actual ulceration, if they are present for some time. Vomiting is a constant symptom, varying in frequency with the degree of gastritis present. Disinclination to feed is also seen, to a greater or lesser extent, and the temperature will be 39–39.5°C (102–103.5°F). Some dogs may have stones in their stomachs for quite a time, large dogs, such as German Shepherds and Airedales, being the worst offenders. Surgery is the only method of removing the foreign bodies. Mixture 1 (see Appendix, p. 84) given frequently and in small amounts will lessen, if not stop, the vomiting and prevent further damage to the delicate wall of the stomach.

Intestines

In the first part of the intestines small stones and bits of bone become lodged. A foreign body in the intestines is serious. In this position a complete obstruction is caused and food cannot pass through the tube-like intestine. By pressure of the muscles of the gut, and owing to the small size of the gut cavity, a spasm of the muscle results, and very soon a congestion of local blood vessels ends in necrosis or gangrene of the intestinal wall. There is always a local peritonitis present, and this, if rupture or puncture of the intestinal walls occurs, rapidly results in a generalised peritonitis. Surgical measures are required as soon as possible. Symptoms are: vomiting (within half to one hour of being fed), temperature is 39°C (102.5°F) or more, the back is arched, the dog has a tucked-up appearance, a tight skin, and signs of abdominal pain. (See also Abdominal Pain, p. 14.)

Whenever a foreign body is suspected NEVER give castor oil or any other purgative. Such dosing will generally ensure that your dog dies an agonising death within twenty-four hours.

Intestinal intussusception, a condition seen particularly in young dogs or puppies of the long-backed breeds (e.g., Dachshunds), has symptoms similar to those of an intestinal foreign body. In this con-dition a portion of intestine passes into a lower part of the adjoining intestine. In other words, the animal tries to pass a bit of its own intes-tine. This is often predisposed to by an enteritis (see Diarrhoea, p. 27). It is seen mainly in puppies or young dogs. The blood supply of the inverted part becomes obstructed, and the intestinal cavity is eliminated completely. Local peritonitis, vomiting and straining, together with abdominal discomfort and a temperature rise of one or more degrees, are signs of this condition, and prompt surgery is indicated. Speed is all the more essential because of the extreme youth of the patient. In such cases *small* amounts of Mixture 1 (see Appendix, p. 84) may be given until a veterinary surgeon has examined the dog.

Rectum

Small fragments of bone may become lodged in the rectum. These can often be felt by gently inserting a carefully greased finger. Restraint such as a muzzle tape (p. 6) may be required to perform this examin-ation. They are also evidenced by the animal's behaviour. Intense pain during the passing of a motion, or inability to perform this task; straining, or probably a little blood-stained faeces; all are symptoms.

The veterinary surgeon usually employs a general anaesthetic to ensure easy removal of the object; this not only frees the animal from pain but also stops the spasm of the anal sphincter, the very strong muscle surrounding the end of the rectum. Do not give a purgative, or an enema, in such cases. If you are certain of the cause of the trouble, and can feel the bone via rectum, a sedative may be given before the dog is seen by a veterinary surgeon, but if this is done he must be informed.

Fractures

General. Fractures are the result of injury to the normally firm skeletal tissue – bone. Fractures may be of three main types:

1. Simple fracture. The bone is broken in one place and there is little displacement (i.e. little disrupture of surrounding tissues, and the broken ends remain fairly close together).
2. Multiple fractures – the bone is fractured in more than one place.
3. Compound fracture – the fracture involves gross displacement or damage to surrounding tissues, the broken ends are not in alignment and may even be protruding through the skin.

39

It will be seen that the compound fracture is by far the most serious. Not only is there displacement of the broken ends but if the skin is broken the bone tissue may be contaminated by dirt and bacteria.

It should always be remembered that a fracture, or a suspected fracture, should be attended to by a veterinary surgeon as promptly as possible. Some fractures (e.g. those affecting ribs, joints, and deep tissues like the pelvis) can be diagnosed only by examining the injured area by X-rays. With these aids to diagnosis the treatment can be carried out more accurately, and the owner given a better idea of the final outcome.

Whilst doctors have the advantage of being able to order a patient with a fractured pelvis to lie on his back in a plaster cast for two or three months the veterinary surgeon must adapt his treatment to his less co-operative, but frequently more sensible, patient. Therefore we find that, in the wide field of fractures, anaesthetics, either local or general, are extensively used. We find that new techniques have been evolved to 'fix' the broken bones in position, such as bone-pinning and the Stader splint. In addition, in compound fractures, where there has been damage to, and possible infection of, the bone tissue itself antibiotics such as penicillin and streptomycin are widely used. Some fractures, typically those of certain parts of the pelvis, are impossible to splint or pin and these may therefore heal only with enforced rest and time, and certain special aids.

First-aid in cases of fractures can be important indeed, and if carried out properly it may prevent a simple fracture becoming a compound one. Common sense and a little knowledge can also prevent or lessen the extent of infection in cases of compound fracture. *First-aid measures* are:

Simple fracture and multiple fractures

The first requirement in a fracture case is to give support to the injured limb. This will prevent displacement of the broken ends, aid subsequent healing, limit shock, pain, and haemorrhage. To attain this end, the limb should be fixed or supported in as near the natural alignment or position as is possible. Simple fractures are commonest in the long bones, i.e. the main bones of the limbs, and the best support is given by splints. Frequently these must of necessity be simple as available materials may be crude and inadequate. A suitably shaped stick tied in position by two handkerchiefs may be a rough support but it may help greatly in preventing further injury. A flat lath or ruler lightly bandaged in position is quite a good support.

To apply a splint, gently bring the limb into as natural a position as possible, lay the support along the limb in the most comfortable and natural position (e.g. in the fore-leg along the front of the leg), then apply two bandages firmly but gently, the first at the uppermost extremity of the limb, the second at the bottom. If bandages are not available strips of sheeting or a couple of handkerchiefs may have to suffice. Finally, if practicable bandage the whole limb lightly, entirely enclosing the splint and the limb. Above all, whether it is possible to splint the limb or not, avoid moving the patient as much as possible and avoid leaving the limb without some support, if only a cushion or a supporting hand. Small dogs can be carried of course, the injured limb being supported by one hand.

Compound fractures

First-aid measures in these cases must often be limited to the prevention of contamination by bacteria of the broken ends of the bone or of the skin wound. If the displacement is not great a supporting splint may be applied as in cases of simple fracture, otherwise a clean handkerchief, bandage or pad tied over the area of wounding is the best immediate action to take. Surgical cleaning will have to be done under an anaesthetic in such cases, when the damage can be more easily assessed, and any foreign objects and portions of broken bone or skin removed.

Briefly, the main principles to be followed in all cases of fracture or suspected fracture are:

1. Keep the damaged area in as near a natural position as possible.
2. If possible, give permanent support to maintain this position, i.e. a splint.
3. Avoid movement of the damaged area and, above all, do not knock or jar it against anything.
4. If there is any skin wound, keep it quite clean. Do *not* bathe this unless you are sure it is only skin deep.

Haemorrhage

Bleeding, when it is from the skin, is a natural process to wash bacteria and dirt from a damaged area. However, it can be dangerous if it is coming from a cut artery or vein, if it comes from the lungs or an internal organ, or from a highly vascular area (i.e. one well supplied with blood vessels). Examples of the latter are the tongue and, in the male dog, the penis.

When blood is noticed from the nose, mouth or anus give nothing by mouth. Keep the patient warm and quiet until attended to by a veterinary surgeon. (See also Accidents, p. 19. For Ear injuries, see p. 30.)

For ordinary wounds on limbs a clean bandage, tied over the injury firmly but not too tightly, will soon stop local bleeding. Bathing with cold water will also steady or stop local haemorrhage. Cold water is certainly of value in cases of injury to the penis. Ice packs or cold water swabs laid on the sheath will soon ease the flow of blood, which can be dangerous if no action is taken.

Arterial haemorrhage. When an artery is severed haemorrhage is profuse. The blood comes in regular gushing spouts, bright red in colour, and in such cases prompt action is necessary to prevent a severe and possibly dangerous loss of blood. A bandage or handkerchief should be tied tightly above the point of haemorrhage; severed arteries are usually on a limb and therefore bandaging can be managed quite adequately. When this has been done, tie another bandage or handkerchief firmly over the wound itself.

These measures will control or stop the bleeding until the animal is properly attended to by a veterinary surgeon.

Venous haemorrhage, or bleeding from a severed vein, is not so severe as with arterial bleeding. Blood will well out often quite rapidly but not in spurts. The haemorrhage is darkish in colour, and not the bright red of arterial bleeding. The limb should be firmly bandaged over the bleeding area and if this does not stem the flow of blood within a few minutes a second bandage should be tied tightly immediately below the injury. This latter bandage should be slowly loosened after 10–15 minutes if help has not come by then. If the bleeding re-starts, apply this bandage again. The bandage over the actual wound should be touched only by the veterinary surgeon, unless it should slip before he arrives.

All cases of arterial or venous haemorrhage should be kept still, warm and quiet.

Hard-pad. (Acute). See Brain, Inflammation of (p. 23) and Hysteria (p. 44).

Heart Attacks

Heart attacks are not as common in dogs as in humans, but they occasionally occur, mostly in very old dogs. Heat-stroke is one main cause of this type of collapse (see p. 26) but in susceptible animals a variety of minor states might predispose or cause an attack. Generally speaking, over-fat dogs are most subject to heart conditions. Animals which have suffered previous heart, lung, liver or kidney disease or injury, are also potential cases of heart failure, or embarrassment.

Treatment. Remove predisposing cause if possible, e.g. if from overheating, remove to cool room. Open the mouth to ensure adequate ventilation and air-intake, and if the animal is unconscious the tongue should be drawn out of the mouth as far as is possible. Lie the animal on its right side, with the head lower than the rest of the body. A little ammonia or smelling-salts held within a few inches of the nose will stimulate by reflex action respiration and heart action. A *few drops* of neat brandy placed on the back of the tongue will also help. Keep the patient absolutely quiet, and if at all cold cover the body with a blanket and place a hot-water bottle or bottles along the spine. Do not cover the head at all and keep a free area at this end to ensure that the patient can breathe freely. Cleaning the mouth with cottonwool soaked in cold water has a stimulating effect and can be repeated frequently. Allow no water to trickle down the throat as in an unconscious animal this may enter the windpipe.

In some mild forms of heart attacks the animal remains conscious and quite sensible. There is in such cases, however, a shortness of breath, panting, probably a staggering gait, and the gums and tongue may appear bluish or cyanosed.

Cases of heart attack usually regain consciousness within 2–5 minutes of the attack but are often too weak to stand for half an hour or so afterwards. Any exertion must be avoided, and it is as well for someone to sit with the animal to prevent it fretting and trying to exert itself unnecessarily. Whilst such cases are not likely to be curable, your veterinary surgeon will be able to prescribe suitable stimulants and advise on diet and handling, or suggest the best course to be adopted. It is important to make sure that the heart is the real cause of the trouble; disease of several other organs can produce conditions resembling these conditions.

However, with adjusted management, stimulants and careful attention to diet, most heart cases may go on quite happily for an amazingly long time.

Heat-stroke

This is most frequent in short-nosed dogs, especially bulldogs. Immediate action is important as collapse and heart failure may occur quite rapidly. Remove the dog to as cool a spot as possible. The animal should be carried and not allowed to exert itself in any way. A room with a stone floor is ideal, and the animal should be laid on its right side with the left side uppermost. A current of air helps greatly, and fanning the dog will increase the intake of fresh air. The head and back of the neck should be douched with cold water, or, if ice is available, an ice pack or compress applied. The mouth should be sponged out with cottonwool or a handkerchief wrung out in cold water, and saliva wiped away so far as is possible. If the animal has collapsed, smelling-salts or ammonia solution held within an inch or two of the nose will often help. A few drops of brandy on the tongue, then a thorough swabbing of the throat to remove the mass of saliva which accumulates and which the collapsed animal is unable to get rid of himself. The patient must be kept absolutely quiet for about half an hour after his recovery, or until he has been examined by a veterinary surgeon, as exertion might result in damage to the strained and fatigued heart.

Hysteria[1]

Hysteria is a temporary mental disturbance seen mainly in puppies and young dogs. Though the symptoms are distressing to the observer the animal itself does not experience any pain and usually emerges from the fit none the worse. Symptoms vary considerably. The animal may run about barking and violently crashing into objects in its path, or it may merely wander, twitch spasmodically, froth at the mouth, and then appear quite normal.

The causes of hysteria and 'fits' are as varied as the forms in which a dog is affected. The usual causes in young dogs are the teething process, indigestion (usually associated with worms, or a dietary indiscretion) or a sudden severe fright. Distemper and/or hard-pad are diseases characterised by mental disturbances of one sort or another, but in such cases other symptoms will almost invariably have preceded the mental stage of the illness. Such symptoms as a cough, discharge from eyes and nose, and diarrhoea, are typical of distemper or hard-pad and animals with these symptoms are usually seen by a veterinary surgeon before any brain complications occur. (See also Brain, Inflammation of, p. 23.)

It should be remembered that until the cause is removed or remedied the hysteria is likely to recur. As this is essentially a first-aid book it is not intended to discuss the differential diagnosis of the many causes of hysteria. That is the expert's field. Important first measures can, however, be taken by the owner of a dog suddenly showing hysteria, and these should be taken promptly.

[1] See also Rabies (p. 66).

44

A dog with a plaster cast on a fractured leg

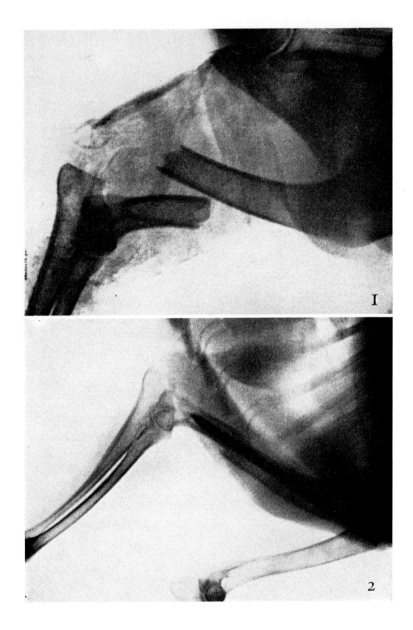

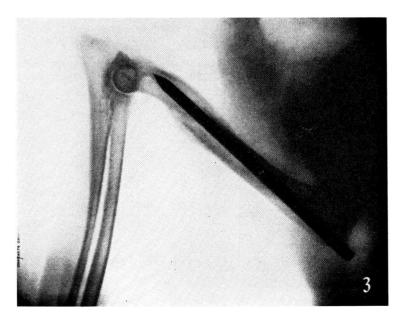

1. This dog has been injured in a street accident. There is a complete fracture of the humerus.

2. The same case two weeks later after a stainless steel pin has been inserted and the fracture reduced under general anaesthesia.

3. The same case two weeks later. Healing is taking place at the site of the break. When this was complete the pin was removed.

Hare Spy, racing with a plastic bone in her hock, wins a race

(P.A.-Reuter)

Remove the animal to a darkened, quiet room where it can do no harm to itself. Fires are dangerous. A dog in its semi-demented state may fall on to one and suffer serious injury.

Keep the animal absolutely quiet and still until the fit or hysteria passes. Precautions should be taken when handling a dog showing hysteria as it may snap or bite unknowingly. Therefore do not handle the head until the fit has passed.

When normal, any of the following should then be given, preferably crushed and administered in a little milk:

½–2 Veganin (according to size of dog), e.g. 12 kilo (30 lb) dog 1 tablet.

OR 3–10 gr. bromide (according to size of dog), e.g. 12 kilo (30 lb) dog 5 gr.

OR a suitable sedative or tranquilliser as prescribed by your veterinary surgeon.

These dosages may be repeated every 1½–2 hours, or earlier if necessary. In the absence of any of these sedatives, give 1 or 2 Paracetamol tablets BP in a little warmed milk, with ½–1 teaspoonful of brandy added. It is again stressed that rest and absolute quiet are most important as any sudden disturbance is likely to start the hysteria afresh.

It is fortunately true that although with hysteria the animal seems terribly distressed during the actual attack he appears to have no memory of his experiences during the upset. In actual fact the owner is generally more disturbed than the animal.

Inhalations

These can be exceedingly unpopular with canine patients but are nevertheless prescribed quite frequently for catarrhal infections, such as are found in distemper.

A narrow vessel (for example, a jug or stone jar) is well warmed in the oven, rinsed out with boiling water and refilled with boiling water plus the medicament chosen. This is usually Friar's Balsam or eucalyptus. Friar's Balsam may stain the vessel so eucalyptus (one teaspoonful to the pint) is preferable. Hold the dog's head over the steam so that he inhales it. The animal must be held firmly throughout (usually for periods of 3–5 minutes, two, three or four times a day) in case he scalds himself.

Another excellent method of treatment by inhalation is the

old-fashioned bronchitis kettle. This resembles an ordinary kettle but the spout is about two feet long. The kettle should be kept boiling on a small stove or spirit-lamp and the spout directed to the dog's bed. A tea-chest placed on its side with wire over the front so that the dog cannot get out makes a splendid 'steam tent' for a small patient. Travelling boxes can be adapted for this purpose. The kettle should be placed near the box with the spout directed at the opening, and a rug can be thrown over part of the front in order to concentrate the vapour. One or two teaspoonfuls of Friar's Balsam can be added to the water in the kettle. This treatment should be carried out for about 10 minutes at a time, and repeated 2 or 3 times daily.

Nasal drops are sometimes prescribed. Most of these act by contracting the blood vessels in the lining of the nose, thereby reducing the inflammation and congestion. The dog's head should be tilted well back and a medicine dropper, procurable from any chemist, is often preferable to the one supplied with the drops, which is sometimes rather large for easy insertion into a dog's small nostrils.

Invalids, Diet for

This subject has already been touched upon under various headings (e.g. Fevers, Feeding in, p. 35).

Diet for a sick or convalescent dog should be light, palatable and nourishing. Broadly speaking, there is no necessity to feed dogs at night as uninterrupted sleep will be of far more benefit.

It would obviously be a mistake, however, for the stomach to be overloaded with one or two large meals with which the digestive organs are unable to deal, so several small meals should be given. Milk, although very nourishing and a great stand-by, is not always suitable by itself and may have to be modified with Benger's. Sometimes milk food made from one of the powdered full-cream infant foods is relished when ordinary milk fails to appeal. Baked custards (made with eggs) are usually much appreciated. Unless contra-indicated, glucose can be added to all milky dishes. As it requires no digestion before assimilation it is a very valuable food.[1] Farex, milk puddings, crushed cornflakes and milk and Brand's Essence are all useful items in invalid diet. Brand's Essence is of particular value in cases of weakness, debility and prostration, and where there is vomiting and diarrhoea Mixture 2 (*see* Appendix, p. 84) will be found excellent.

---

[1] Honey is also recommended. See footnote p. 35.

When diarrhoea is present feed the dog as advised in the section on Diarrhoea (p. 27).

White fish boiled in milk, raw chopped meat in very small quantities and boiled rabbit can be given in convalescence. Eggs are more easily digested when given beaten up with milk, lightly boiled, or in custards. Barley water is best in kidney cases. Some of the lighter breakfast foods – cornflakes, rice crisps, and so on – bridge the gap between very light invalid food and more solid diet. The change from one to the other should always be gradual, particularly where there has been diarrhoea and vomiting.

Sometimes strong black coffee or brandy mixed with milk is advised when prostration or collapse is present.

Do not be tempted to give too much at one time – a sick dog should have only a few teaspoonsful every two or three hours. Keep spoons and dishes very clean and never leave food in the sick-room.

Avoid rich, indigestible foods such as herrings and sardines. Obviously dog biscuit should not be given. Rusks or lightly baked brown bread make a good substitute as convalescence progresses.

Dietary supplements containing vitamins are particularly important to the convalescent animal. The most necessary vitamins at this time are A, B complex and D. A comprehensive supplement such as Stress is the best way of supplying these essential factors. Fresh raw or lightly cooked liver is a rich source of the vitamin B complex. If liver is used be sure that it is absolutely fresh, and if such a supply is unobtainable one of the very good liver extracts on the market may be used instead. Do not use dried liver or liver meal.

Mastitis – Acute

Mastitis, or inflammation of a milk gland, is usually seen in bitches in milk. Therefore this condition arises in bitches which have recently whelped, or less commonly, in those which have had a false or 'phantom' pregnancy (i.e. all the changes of pregnancy have occurred but no puppies have been produced). In cases of mastitis the milk gland or glands affected are hot, hard and tense, being painful to the touch, and the milk secretion is discoloured. The condition may mature quite rapidly – in 12 or 24 hours – so it is important that expert attention be given as soon as possible. Temperature usually reaches $39.5–40.5°C(103–105°F)$, and the bitch shows signs of pain, refuses food and develops an excessive thirst. There may or may not be vomiting, and pain sometimes causes the bitch to snap at her young if they attempt to feed from the affected gland.

47

Before skilled help arrives steps can be taken to prevent the condition becoming worse. The gland should be well fomented with warm water or warm olive oil, and any secretions gently milked out by a gentle squeezing with finger and thumb towards the teat. This can be repeated every hour. The procedure greatly helps to relieve the local congestion and prevent any further absorption of poisons from the gland.

This condition should not be confused with that of mammary tumour, which shows itself as a swelling in one or more of the milk glands, usually in the bitch when not in milk. The swelling is usually painless, hard, and localised to a portion of a gland. The temperature remains normal and the bitch's general health is unchanged. Professional advice should be sought in such cases but great urgency is not present.

The prevention of mastitis. This inflammation of the mammary glands in the bitch, which arises from various causes, is sometimes avoidable. The most important cause is injury from the puppies or from some other source, or an accumulation of milk in one gland due to it having been neglected for some reason by the offspring.

It is essential to cut the points of the puppies' nails from ten days of age onwards about once a week; these grow at astonishing speed and can lacerate the glands. Pekingese and other low-to-the-ground bitches should have the top of the whelping box very smooth otherwise injuries can be caused when getting in and out.

An accumulation of milk can be prevented by feeling all the glands regularly, making sure they are soft and pliable, and encouraging the puppies to suck from all the teats. If a gland begins to feel full and hard the milk must be drawn off by hand several times a day until the gland is soft. Vaseline or olive oil will help to keep it in a supple condition. Any hardness or fullness is often the preliminary to mastitis which, like all local inflammatory conditions, shows the classic signs of heat, pain and swelling. Mastitis is usually preventable and should not occur if a bitch is properly cared for by an observant owner.

Mastitis is sometimes found in bitches who have lost all their litter and have plenty of milk. Such cases are more difficult to prevent and if it is possible to use the bitch as a foster, this should be done. A bitch deprived of her puppies can become ill with misery, quite apart from discomfort from her milk. If this is impossible to remedy, the bitch must be returned to normal as quickly as possible by giving her very dry food and mostly biscuit (not meat), Epsom salts internally, and by careful observation of her glands. They should not be touched, if touching is avoidable, as massage increases the supply of milk. Sometimes treatment with an oestrogen becomes necessary, and sedatives are often required. The owner must be very watchful and call in veterinary assistance immediately if the bitch seems restless, distressed and anxious, and if she is feverish or shows symptoms of mastitis.

Mésalliance

Mésalliance, or accidental mating of the in-season bitch, is a frequent mishap and is often regarded by the owner as a major disaster, especially if the animal has a pedigree. If the bitch is found at time of actual mating no attempt should be made to separate her from the dog. By that time interference will only add the risk of injury to the bitch, and this may result in severe bruising or even tearing of the vagina. Such damage may have permanent results.

As soon as the animals have parted your veterinary surgeon should be consulted. Douching of the vagina by the owner should not be attempted; unless this is done by a skilled person injury or infection may occur. Also, this course is not generally effective in preventing the unwanted litter. The hormone injection is effective in the majority, if not in all, cases of mésalliance. It does not in any way harm the bitch's powers of reproduction at a later date. It is important, however, that the injection be given within a reasonable time of the accidental mating; a delay of over forty-eight hours is likely to reduce the efficiency of the injection considerably.

Incidentally, the fallacy of 'tainting', or marking of subsequent pedigree litters by a mating with a mongrel dog, has been quite conclusively disproved and has no scientific basis.

It is of course impossible to breed from the bitch at the season when the mésalliance occurs if a hormone injection has been given.

Milk, lack of, in Nursing Bitches

A very trying condition which may be partial or complete. Sometimes it is due to insufficient protein (e.g. raw meat) and when this is the case plenty of raw meat should be given and a generous allowance of warm milk. When this has no effect your veterinary surgeon may be able to help. A hormone injection is now available which has been successfully used for this condition. It is administered hypodermically and should be given as soon as possible after whelping.

A gentle massage of the milk glands with a little warm olive oil will also stimulate the blood supply to the area, and thereby increase the glands' ability to produce milk. This is also useful in cases of over-hard or distended milk glands when *no* infection is present. (For Mastitis, see p. 47).

Nails – Broken

Broken nails are common, particularly in the sporting breeds, when the dew claws have not been removed. Breaking or tearing of the nail does, however, occur on the toes as well, and involves one of two areas. The tear may be at the base of the nail, when the whole of the nail is torn from its attachment to the toe and is usually left hanging by a portion of skin. Alternatively, the break may occur halfway down the body of the nail, the root remaining firmly attached to the skin at the base of the claw. In both types of injury it is usual for the broken end to be left attached to the body portion. This portion should not be pulled or any attempt made to remove it – although the point of attachment may appear small it is usually quite tough, and the pain caused by touching the broken claw is considerable. Gentle bathing with warm water containing a little non-irritant antiseptic should be the first step. Then a pad of cottonwool or gauze should be placed over the injured claw, taking care to keep the broken portion in line with the rest of the toe. A bandage over this pad will ensure that the injured end is kept clean and free from jarring until the broken portion can be removed. This should be done by the veterinary surgeon, who may have to employ a local anaesthetic.

A pair of nail clippers may be used if the break is near the free end of the nail and a sharp snip just over the break will often sever the broken end quickly and painlessly. A clean dressing should be kept on for several days until the broken end has healed. It is important that this should be done as dirt and grit can enter the wound and cause a secondary infection, which will greatly delay healing.

Nasal Discharge

The nose, in health, is always moist, and by a discharge we mean one which is clearly perceptible, whether water or mucopurulent. In the former case there is the perpetual 'dew-drop' at the end of the nose, often seen in hard-pad. It should not be confused with the occasional 'drip' seen in nervous puppies when handled by strangers.

A nasal discharge is due to a variety of causes which may be summarised as local and general.

When the cause is local it may be due to a small foreign body (e.g. a grass seed), to breathing heavily polluted air (for example, when an oil-stove smokes), to some strictly local infection or to a congenital abnormality. When the cause is general it is associated with disease – for example, distemper.

The temperature should be taken. If normal, and the dog is cheerful, it is probably a local trouble. Sometimes, even when there is no general illness, the dog is depressed and hangs his head; this is often due to a headache and a Paracetamol tablet will bring much relief. When the dog has a slight temperature 39°C (102.5°F) upwards, the eyes are inflamed and reddened with or without a slight discharge, and he seems a little depressed and perhaps disinclined to eat, it is probable that the nasal discharge is a symptom of one of the virus infections, such as hard-pad.

Unless the cause is obvious (for instance, the smoking stove mentioned above) a nasal discharge in a previously healthy dog always needs investigation if it persists for more than a few hours. A veterinary surgeon should be consulted and, if describing the condition by telephone the type of discharge (clear and watery or thick and purulent) should be mentioned, whether slight or profuse, when it began, the dog's general state of health, and whether there is any possible reason. For example, if a dog has been taken for a walk in fields of uncut hay, grass seeds may be responsible.

Do not touch or wipe off the discharge until the veterinary surgeon has examined the dog.

Purulent Nasal Discharge, Removal of
When the cause of the trouble has been diagnosed and treatment begun, the owner can make the animal far more comfortable, and certainly more presentable, by regular removal of the discharge every two or three hours. The veterinary surgeon may advise inhalations (see p. 45) or nasal drops, and the latter may cause sneezing and so help to remove the accumulated matter as dogs cannot blow their own noses!

The nostrils should be cleaned very gently with cottonwool wound round a match-stick and dipped in warm water with a very mild antiseptic (TCP answers well for this purpose). Discard each piece of cottonwool after using once and introduce the match-stick into each nostril with the greatest gentleness. Finish with dry wool. Sometimes pure olive oil is better than water. After cleaning the nose in this way smear a little vaseline over the surface and under the flaps of the nostrils, which are apt to get stuck down with the discharge.

All swabs used for cleaning should be burnt immediately. (For Nasal drops (how to administer) see Inhalations, p. 46.)

Operation Cases, After-care of

The care of post-operative cases will depend to a large extent on the nature and severity of the operation, and whether surgical measures have been carried out as the culmination of a long, serious illness or in an animal whose general condition is excellent. Constitutional disturbance is either absent or very slight where a minor operation is performed (i.e. to correct inverted eyelids) but may be very great in a serious abdominal condition. If the animal needs much in the way of skilled attention – difficult dressings, stimulants, and so on – he will probably be kept at the veterinary hospital or clinic as long as these are required. Similarly, if the dog's post-operative condition is such that removal would be dangerous he will be kept until it is safe for him to return to his owner. Dogs, particularly pet dogs, usually recover more quickly at home, and veterinary surgeons for this reason try to return an animal as speedily as possible. The anxious amateur nurse may have the dog's care on her hands sooner than she imagined!

If feasible, she should try to find out at the hospital whether the dog has to be kept as much at rest as possible, and what his general condition is. Dogs, unlike human patients, are not confined to bed as a rule after an operation unless they are so weak or shocked that rest and quiet are essential, in which case they will be kept in hospital. Movement within reason is beneficial, and recent research has shown that human patients, too, are often better if exercise is encouraged from the start. The ideal bedding for a post-operative case is Vetbed – excellent and far superior to blankets.

Diet in post-operation cases. Diet should be light and confined to fluids for a few days, and glucose or honey should be added to all drinks. There is always loss of blood with which to contend; shock may still be present in a mild degree and fluid mixed with glucose will do much to remedy this. The return to normal diet should be gradual by way of such light, easily digested fare as baked custards, white fish boiled in milk, brown bread and milk, lightly boiled eggs, etc. Cod liver oil and malt is excellent for convalescent patients, whether medical or surgical.

When solid diet is permitted this should be especially nourishing – for instance, four meals a day; breakfast of cereal and milk; for midday feed, a generous allowance of raw meat or boiled rabbit plus wholemeal and halibut oil and vitamin supplement; for tea, an egg beaten up in milk, and for the evening meal, raw meat or fish. These body-building foods (or proteins, as we call them) – meat, fish, milk and eggs – are needed to replace the protein being used by the body to repair the injured tissues. In much the same way the nursing and expectant bitch is fed liberally with these protein foods to help her to replace her own 'body builders' which are being used for the growth and nourishment of her puppies.

Dressing the Wound

As the wound will normally be aseptic the original dressing should not need renewal unless the veterinary surgeon particularly wishes it. There is, however, sometimes discharge from the wound and these cases will, of course, need to be dressed, although usually gentle removal of the discharge with clean cottonwool and warm boiled water is all that is required.

When dressing an operation wound everything used to touch it should be sterilised (i.e. rendered free from bacteria) by boiling beforehand. Cottonwool, broken up into small swabs, should be boiled in a scrupulously clean covered saucepan and the water used for this when cooled, will be useful for removing any discharge. Remember that the water will stay sterile only if the lid is firmly on. A piece of lint sufficiently large to cover the wound should be cut from a packet of sterilised lint (this is obtainable from the chemist), using scissors which have been boiled. If an antibiotic powder or any other dressing is to be applied, have this in a screw-topped jar or sealed container kept tightly covered except when actually in use, and boil the teaspoon used for applying the powder. It is advisable to use forceps, also sterilised, to handle the cottonwool swabs used for wiping away the discharge, but in any case the hands should be thoroughly scrubbed with plenty of soap and water. Have everything ready on a tray beforehand – the covered saucepan with the cottonwool swabs in the warm boiled water, the scissors, the piece of lint (which should be left covered up in its packet until the last moment), the spoon and powder (if this is ordered), bandages and/or surgical coat and a receptacle for the soiled dressings. Have the scissors, forceps and spoon in the saucepan in which they have been sterilised immersed in the boiled water until you need to use them; if left uncovered they will quickly become contaminated by germs in the atmosphere.

If the soiled dressing adheres to the wound it must never be pulled off; a little of the warmed boiled water should be trickled between the dressing and wound until the dressing can be gently removed. *Never* touch the wound with your fingers if you can avoid doing so, and preferably use forceps for handling the wool to wipe away the discharge. Be careful to wipe the latter away from the wound and not across it. Do not have the cottonwool any wetter than necessary.

Occasionally it may be necessary for the veterinary surgeon to remove a suture (stitch) to allow drainage, and if the wound appears

53

very red and swollen in one part, with no discharge, he should be informed. The sutures are removed about a week after the operation and it is a wise precaution to take the temperature daily for about five days. Any rise to 39°C (102.5°F) and over should be reported. The animal should wear a surgical coat until healing is complete and dressings may have to be continued for some days after the removal of the sutures.

Most post-operative cases need plenty of rest and quiet; even if the dog seems to be little affected, any surgical interference is a shock to the system and the animal needs a peaceful convalescence.

Surgical Coats, How to Make

Surgical coats, used for protecting wounds (particularly abdominal) after operations, should be made from clean, strong white material (old sheeting is usually very suitable). Four holes should be made for the legs, the material drawn up and fastened along the back and round the neck, and shaped where necessary over the thighs. Perfect fitting is not necessary provided the coat prevents the dog from licking at his wound or worrying at the bandages. He should be able to move comfortably. When shaping, be careful with the scissors as it is easy to cut off too much material. Here and there a few stiches can be inserted to keep the coat tidy and it should be fastened by tapes (never safety pins) along the back. At least three coats should be made to allow for accidental soiling and regular laundering.

Pads, Cracked

When a dog limps and the pad is cracked the only way to cure the condition is to protect the dog's foot during healing. A piece of lint sufficiently large to cover the pads should be smeared thickly with boracic ointment and secured as follows: a length of 'Sleek' plaster should be taken from just below the pastern (or kneee) joint over the foot and up the back while the dog is standing on the foot. Secure this by bandaging in the ordinary way round the leg and foot with more plaster. This, if efficiently done, makes a secure, neat and immovable covering, that can be left until it drops off naturally. Although dogs make the most determined efforts to chew the strapping off they will find this impossible if the bandaging has been properly done.

Paralysis

This condition, a symptom or result rather than a disease in itself, is tedious to nurse and alarming to see, but even apparently hopeless cases can sometimes make remarkable recoveries. Paralysis can be caused by acute constipation bringing with it auto-intoxication, but the remedy for this is simple and when the cause is treated the paralysis disappears. In distemper and hard-pad, and in some other serious diseases affecting the central nervous system, paralysis is fairly common. The veterinary surgeon will of course, always be informed at its onset, which is shown by weakness, staggering, and stiffness of the hindquarters. It can involve the whole body but more usually it is the hindquarters which are affected. The dog is unable to stand but drags his legs behind him when he tries to move. The bowels are constipated and the bladder may share in the general paralysis although later there may be incontinence. When the brain is seriously affected the dog will lie completely helpless, unable to lift more than his head.

The bowels and bladder must receive attention to begin with, as elimination is always of vital importance in these cases, and constipation can make the condition much worse. If not otherwise directed, Epsom salts are useful and an enema can be given if the salts do not operate in a few hours. If the dog is supported standing and his flanks are gently pressed, the bladder may be emptied successfully. This should be repeated two or three times a day. Failing this, it may be necessary to pass a catheter, but as this can be dangerous in unskilled hands it is a job for the veterinary surgeon. A cloth wrung out in hot water 38°C (100°F) and held to the abdomen between the thighs sometimes helps.

Dogs which are able to walk at all should be encouraged to do so, if necessary supported, unless the veterinary surgeon wants his patient to be kept still. A wide, strong bandage round the abdomen, with a curtain ring sewn to the top and a lead attached, will form a useful sling to support the animal where he needs it and yet give some freedom.

When the dog is absolutely helpless he should be nursed in a smooth, flat, firm bed and turned very hour. Incontinence is an inevitable problem (see p. 9). Warmth for the spine is helpful, so the dog should have a well-covered hot-water bottle placed along his back. Gentle massage and stroking down the length of the spine is often useful. Remember to keep the patient warm, and as a paralysed animal's skin can be easily injured, bruised or broken, be sure that his bed is comfortable. Always handle him very gently and smoothly, and do not forget to turn him regularly. Although paralysis is a trying condition to nurse, and sometimes takes a long time, the animal has a good chance of complete recovery provided that the nervous system is not permanently damaged. No one should be in a hurry to have an animal destroyed unless the veterinary surgeon in attendance advises that the case is hopeless. In addition, special two-wheeled carts are now available, which, when attached by a comfortable lightweight harness, give a fair degree of mobility to the patient.

Parvovirus, Canine (CPV)

The year 1978 will go down in history as a black one for our canine friends. During that year – apparently quite spontaneously and also near simultaneously – a new disease appeared world-wide. Its cause turned out to be a new or hitherto unidentified organism, now known as canine parvovirus (CPV). The appearance of this infection in a short period of time, on a near world-wide basis, can only emphasise the futility of man-made boundaries and, for that matter, disease control procedures against new and unknown viruses. After it was identified it was proven to be a close cousin of a virus already identified in cats, and called the feline panleucopaenia virus. How the canine cousin arose is largely conjecture, but it could be a genetic variant which adapted to dogs (if so it is the first time this is known to happen), or it could have resulted from an aberrant strain of the panleucopaenia virus as an unwelcome 'passenger' in the tissue culture vaccine production of some canine virus or other organism of dogs.

While its precise origin will remain remote for probably a long time, if not for ever, its unwelcome and dangerous spread produced death and disease in thousands of dogs. The symptoms take two main forms: the enteric and the myocardial types. In the enteric type an acute and non-responsive enteritis is seen, with a profuse and dehydrating diarrhoea. This form can affect all ages of dogs but it is particularly severe and dangerous in young puppies.

The second type of CPV symptoms, the myocardial, is seen when the virus produces acute heart muscle damage, and is less common than the enteric form. It is more frequently seen in the very young puppy and the unprotected young dog under one year of age.

Infection would seem to be mainly by the mouth, from faeces, and faecally contaminated food or water, and three to five days later, except in the per-acute myocardial type, an elevated temperature and acute diarrhoea are seen.

As the upper part of the small intestine is where the CPV is found in greatest concentration, and where it does most of its damage, then vomiting is also a frequent symptom. This inevitably adds to the dehydration, and fluid therapy, both by transfusion and by mouth, will help in the treatment of this infection, which is otherwise governed by treating the symptoms as and when they appear.

Vaccination, as with all infectious diseases, is the ultimate answer and vaccines specifically prepared from strains of the CPV from dogs are now widely available.

Live or dead vaccines can be used, but in view of some of the imponderables which have yet to be investigated more fully the majority of veterinary surgeons favour the dead vaccines, arguing that at least with these no new mutations can arise as could conceivably happen with a live attenuated virus vaccine. On the other hand the pro-live virus vaccine veterinarians point out that a live vaccine will produce a better immunity response. It is best to be guided by your own veterinary surgeon when you take your puppy or dog along to him or her to have the vaccinal procedures started. One thing is certain, in parvovirus, we have another example of Nature's unpredictability, and a re-emphasis of the lesson that we can never relax in our fight against diseases, old or new.

Placenta, Retained

Retention of a placenta (or puppy-bag) is fortunately not common but may occur on occasions, especially if the whelping has been a protracted or exhausting one, or if there is any uterine disease or abnormality.

Retention is not usually suspected until 2–3 days later. If the temperature is taken daily following whelping a rise to 39.5°C (103°F) or more will be seen. Occasionally, however, an observant owner may notice a little membrane-like strand protruding from the vulva after whelping. When the placenta, or a portion, has been retained for two or three days the bitch will show a vaginal discharge, often foul-smelling, and a temperature reaction of 39.5–41°C (103–106°F). She will strain intermittently, be listless and unwilling to feed. There will be little milk for the puppies and these will quickly become weak, puling, skinny little objects. The bitch may vomit, and this rapidly becomes more frequent and finally a constant symptom as peritonitis, develops. In such cases small amounts of Mixture 1 (See Appendix, p. 84), may be given repeatedly until qualified help arrives. The owner of a bitch with a suspected retention of the placenta should inform a veterinary surgeon immediately. If a small portion is showing do not attempt to pull or tug at this; a fragment may break off, leaving the rest inside the womb. The best the owner can do is to carry out common-sense treatment. Keep the bitch warm. Give plenty of fluids, e.g. milk and glucose, or water and glucose, and thoroughly clean the vulva and hind parts with a little warm water. This will make the bitch more comfortable and also lessen the possibility of her aggravating her poisoned state by constantly licking up and swallowing any infected discharge.

Retention of the placenta is serious, but with modern antibiotics and hormones at his disposal a veterinary surgeon, if informed promptly, will stand a very good chance of rapidly restoring your animal to full health.

Pneumonia Jackets

These are made on the pattern of surgical coats but a piece of old blanket should be used instead of sheeting. Thermogene wool should be lightly tacked inside, and removed piece by piece when the dog is better. The coat should cover the chest and ribs but need not extend over the abdomen. Like the surgical coat, it should be fastened neatly with tapes.

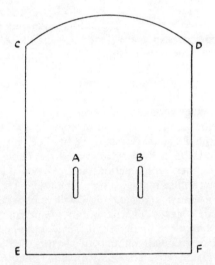

Figure 4
Pattern for Pneumonia Jacket. The puppy's front legs
are put through the holes A and B. Stitch E to F behind
his neck and continue down the back till C meets D.
Never use safety pins

Poisons

Poisoning in dogs is not very common but when it does occur prompt action is required. The subject of poisoning is complex because a number of agents may produce the symptoms of poisoning. These symptoms can be summed up as follows:

Abdominal pain, usually colicky in nature; there may be vomiting, and later diarrhoea. In some types of poisoning nervous symptoms may be seen, particularly where strychnine or the phenols are involved. Collapse, with cold extremities, inability to stand, and stertorous, harsh breathing are the final symptoms.

Immediate Action
In all cases of poisoning, or suspected poisoning, give an emetic. The best is a small lump of washing soda, administered by opening the animal's mouth, dropping the soda on the back of the tongue, and firmly pushing it down the throat with a finger. This procedure should be adopted in all cases of poisoning with one exception. This is in cases of strychnine poisoning, in which the animal has in the later stages convulsive or fit-like movements. In such cases the risk to the owner in opening the mouth and putting a finger inside is too great, as this might bring on a convulsion and clamping of the jaws.

A veterinary surgeon should be consulted promptly in all cases of poisoning and suspected poisoning.

If at all possible, when a suspected poison has been taken in by mouth, save or take with you a sample of this to your veterinary surgeon. Chemical poisons, with all the toxic preparations used in the garden and in farming are a study in themselves, but a clue in the form of a specimen or a container can often save valuable time in attempting to identify the cause of the symptoms.

A few comments on the commonest poisons are alphabetically listed below. For summarised guidance see p. 62.

Arsenic
This is found in some rat poisons. The symptoms are usually vomiting, restlessness, severe abdominal pain, strong desire for water (if allowed, this intensifies the vomiting and increases absorption of the poison).

Barium Chloride
This also is found in certain rat poisons. It produces symptoms of an acute nature – vomiting, diarrhoea and loss of use of the limbs.

Coal Tar, Carbolic (Phenols)

Phenol poisoning may result from several sources. Dogs walking in tar may lick sufficient off their feet to produce acute poisoning. Household disinfectants and carbolic soaps are other causes of trouble, dogs being extraordinarily susceptible to the phenols and very little is required to produce symptoms of poisoning. Symptoms are abdominal pain, twitching and paralysis. Blindness is a fairly constant symptom in an advanced case. If any phenol or tar is still present on the skin, wash this off immediately, as well as giving general treatment, as absorption of the tar from the skin may be quite considerable. Never use carbolic soaps or disinfectant when bathing a dog.

Coal Gas

Often the animal is unconscious. Remove to open air, open the mouth, pull out tongue and apply artificial respiration until help arrives. If the animal is breathing regularly when found, allow plenty of fresh air and give a stimulant, e.g. drops of brandy on tongue, and when sensible, Mixture 2 (see Appendix, p. 84) may be given frequently. The patient should be kept warm and quiet until he has been examined by a veterinary surgeon.

(For Artificial Respiration, see p. 20).

Food Poisoning

There are three main types of food poisoning. Food may contain:

1. Toxins (poisons produced by bacteria).
2. Bacteria (which may produce toxins within the animal's intestines).
3. Chemical poisons or irritants (usually contaminants, or from faulty 'canning').

Toxins

This is the commonest, and also the least serious, of the types of food poisoning. Symptoms are diarrhoea, abdominal pain, and in severe cases the motions may be blood-tinged. Enteritis from toxins in food can be caused by cooked foods as well as by raw. The heating or cooking of food will kill the bacteria or germs present but will not necessarily destroy the toxins they have already produced. Meat is the main offender, and it should therefore always be fresh, cooked immediately, and kept in a cool place in a saucepan with a tightly fitting lid. If any has to be used more than two days later, re-boil. This will help to prevent any trouble.

In cases of enteritis from 'bad' meat give a mild purgative, e.g. ½–2 teaspoonsful castor oil or Epsom salts. A teaspoonful of brandy added to this will alleviate the colicky type. (The purge should be omitted if the dog is very diarrhoeaic, or if dysentery, i.e. blood in motions, is seen.) Thin arrowroot gruel *ad lib* is the best and most readily available treatment. Medicinal charcoal is also useful, and may be given with the arrowroot. The gruel should be substituted for the normal drinking water until the attack has passed. Your veterinary surgeon should be consulted in all cases where blood is seen in the motions, or when the attack has not cleared up within 12 hours.

Bacterial food poisoning

This is a more serious form of enteritis. A certain degree of fever is usually present $39–39.5°C$ ($102.5–103.5°F$). The animal is dejected, and tight skinned. For first-aid measures treat as instructed in previous section. If, however, this type of poisoning is suspected your veterinary surgeon should be consulted immediately as the dog will require medicinal treatment to kill the bacteria, which often establish themselves in the intestines. This type is therefore likely to be more prolonged and need remedies more specific.

It is most important to be scrupulously careful in washing one's hands after dosing, cleaning or nursing such patients as certain types of these bacteria can produce enteritis in humans, if ingested. Salmonella group of organisms fall into this category, so extra care should be taken when handling these patients.

Chemical poisons (food contaminants)

Occasionally food becomes contaminated by a poison or chemical. Paraffin, kerosene, and others are usually so noxious that the animal will refuse the food. Rat poisons sometimes are accidentally mixed with food, in which case the animal should be treated as for the specific poison.

Faulty canning as a cause of chemical poisoning is today most rare, but if such a case is met with, treat as for toxins, but using Epsom salts, not castor oil, as a purge.

Lead Poisoning

This may occur in puppies or dogs which lick, or chew, lead paint covered objects. Symptoms are: abdominal pain, reeling, and finally the dog becomes comatose. *Treatment.* An emetic should be given immediately. When this has acted, give 2 or 3 *small* doses of Epsom salts at ½-hour intervals. Mixture 2 (see Appendix, p. 84) should then be given frequently, as this will make any lead salts left behind insoluble, and therefore harmless.

POISONING SUMMARY

Emetic = lump of washing soda *or* strong solution of salt (sodium chloride)

	ARSENIC	BARIUM CHLORIDE	COAL TAR CARBOLIC ACID (*phenols*)	COAL GAS	FOOD	LEAD	PHOSPHORUS	BARBITURATES	STRYCHNINE
P	1. Emetic.	1. Emetic.	1. Wash off any external phenol, e.g. tar.	1. Artificial respiration.	1. Emetic.	1. Emetic.	1. Emetic.	1. Emetic.	1. Emetic *only* if no convulsions seen.
R	2. Small frequent doses of Epsom salts.	2. Small frequent doses of Epsom salts.	2. Emetic.	2. *Drops* of brandy on tongue.	2. Epsom salts.	2. Epsom salts in small amounts, frequently, by mouth.	2. Permanganate of potash crystals dissolved in water.	2. Stimulants (coffee, brandy).	2. Quiet and sedatives. (Sedatives may be given slowly in liquid form if con-
O									
C	3. Mixture 1 (see Appendix)	3. Stimulants, e.g. weak coffee, brandy.	3. Glauber's salts (½–1 teaspoon-ful) re-	3. Smelling salts.	3. Arrow-root gruel. Mixture 1 if vomiting is persistent (see	3. Mixture 2 frequently (see Appendix)	3. Epsom salts.	3. Constant stimulation noise, moving and	vulsions seen.)
E			peated 2 or 3 times.	4. Glucose by mouth when conscious.	Appendix)		*Avoid* milk, fats.	pinching of patient. Smelling salts.	
D									
U		4. Mixture 1 (see Appendix)	4. Mixture 1 (see Appendix)						
R									
E									

For Metaldehyde and Warfarin poisoning see p. 63.

A veterinary surgeon should be consulted promptly in all cases of poisoning or suspected poisoning.

Metaldehyde Poisoning (Slug Bait)

This particular poison is one which does occur from time to time and in view of the highly dangerous nature of this poison immediate veterinary attention should be sought. If however it is suspected that the dog has eaten some slug bait then an emetic should be given. The main effect of this agent is on the central nervous system of the dog and hyperexcitability is a common feature of poisoning. Your veterinary surgeon will be able to treat this, usually, quite effectively. Always be careful though that these poisons and similar agents used in gardening are put in places inaccessible to animals.

Phosphorus

This is a common constituent of rat poisons, e.g. Rodine. First give an emetic, then small amounts of permanganate of potash crystals dissolved in a little water. Follow this by a dose of Epsom salts, and finally a little glucose in water. Do *not* give any oily purge, or any milk, or other fatty food.

Barbiturates

Occasionally a dog will accidentally eat some phenobarbitone, intended for medicinal purposes, or other types of barbiturate. First give an emetic. Follow this with stimulants, e.g. black coffee, and constant stimulation until a veterinary surgeon sees the case.

Strychnine

This is occasionally put down to kill rats or moles, although its use is strictly controlled by law. The animal will show excitement, and convulsions of a rigid nature, arching the neck and lying stretched out with legs stuck straight out. Give an emetic *only* if *no* convulsions are seen, as these spasms affect the jaws and are uncontrollable, and may therefore result in a severe bite. Quiet is essential and if possible give a large dose of a sedative (see Appendix, p. 85). The animal should be seen by a veterinary surgeon as soon as possible.

Warfarin Poisoning

Warfarin is an agent which is commonly used for killing rats and mice and is even referred to by some people as being harmless to animals. This is quite inaccurate, as Warfarin can produce very severe haemorrhages in dogs should they accidentally take in this poison or should they eat carcases of rats or mice which have died from Warfarin. It is particularly important that if a dog is suspected of having eaten Warfarin or Warfarin contaminated material then an emetic should be given immediately. In addition it is essential that prompt veterinary attention is given to the dog in order to attempt to counteract any of the side effects of the poison.

Puppies, Deaths in Newborn

Sometimes puppies within the first few days of birth begin to whimper continually, lose interest in suckling and do not thrive. If left untreated, they die. This condition is sometimes erroneously ascribed to so-called 'acid milk' in the dam; actually, it is normal for all bitches to have acid milk. Although baby puppies may die from many causes – cold, lack of milk, injury at birth, too long 'on the way', amongst others – when the above symptoms occur they are probably due to a streptococcal or staphylococcal infection. Only immediate measures will be of avail. This naturally requires the attention of the veterinary surgeon as antibiotics may be required.

In addition, many puppies are lost through lack of warmth at whelping time or during the first week or two, so keep the kennel or whelping room very warm, supplying a covered hot-water bottle in the whelping bed in winter.

Every puppy is born in a kind of bag and if this is not broken quickly at the head of the puppy it will die.

When a bitch invariably produces her young very slowly, and the puppies die as a result, parturition can often be 'speeded up' with specific injections. (For Uterine Inertia see Whelping, p. 75.)

Puppies, How to Rear by Hand

When a bitch is unable to rear her family a foster-mother should be obtained if possible. Failing this, the litter must be raised by hand. It is an arduous and exhausting business, but there is no reason why such methods should not succeed if the owner is willing to sacrifice time and sleep. More than one champion has been reared by hand.

Any of the dried milk baby foods can be given, and goat's milk is very good. The ideal, of course, is to have a foster-mother but this is seldom possible.

An especially rich full-cream baby milk food can also be used (a good one is Ostermilk No. 1). This, during feeding, should be kept standing in a basin of hot water to maintain blood heat. It should be mixed to the consistency of condensed milk and then slightly thinned to resemble very rich, creamy cow's milk. Add medicinal glucose (one saltspoonful per puppy for small breeds) and give a teaspoonful or more of the mixture to each puppy, using an old-fashioned medicine dropper with a rubber bulb.[1] It is best to feed each puppy on a covered hot-water bottle; they like to push at it with their feet while drinking. Open the puppy's mouth, put the dropper in and feed *slowly*, allowing time for the little thing to swallow and breathe. He may protest at first but will quickly learn to enjoy it. Be careful not to give too much. The puppies should be fed every two hours during the day and every three hours at night. After ten days the night feeds are cut down to one at midnight, one at 4 a.m., and one at 8 a.m. After a fortnight there is no need to feed at night at all. Adexolin drops (Glaxo) are excellent and should be added to the feeds – one or two drops according to size.

The puppies must be kept very warm and if the dam is able to keep them clean so much the better, otherwise the abdomen should be gently rubbed in a circular action until the bowels have acted, and the puppies kept clean with cottonwool dipped in a mild antiseptic and carefully dried with dry cottonwool. A dusting with boracic powder on abdomen and rear completes the process. At three weeks scraped raw meat can be given, as with the normally reared puppy.

Hand-reared puppies usually thrive if kept very warm and fed regularly and punctually. Keep all utensils, medicine dropper and similar articles scrupulously clean, just as you would do for a human baby.

Pyometra

This is an important and serious condition (pus in the womb) in which the uterus is infected. Although it is usually confined to maiden bitches of 6 years of age or more, it is occasionally seen in young bitches as a result of infection acquired at the time of whelping or contracted from the stud dog. When a bitch is not bred from, the uterine tissues begin to deteriorate in the course of time, and this makes them more likely to become infected with harmful bacteria. In the case of young bitches accidentally infected after mating or whelping there is no degeneration of the uterine tissues, but infection occurs from outside, usually with the commoner groups of micro-organisms. All bitches should have at least one litter, which will, to a large extent, prevent this dangerous condition.

There are two types of pyometra, open and closed, the latter being

---

[1] The Belcroy Tube Feeder (for premature babies) made by Bell & Croyden, Wigmore St, London W1H 0AU, is excellent.

far more acute. The symptoms vary, but fever is always present – 39.5°C (103°F) upwards; there is loss of appetite, vaginal discharge (in the open type) of a brownish or pinkish colour and, as the condition becomes worse, great thirst, frequent vomiting and finally prostration. If untreated, a toxaemia quickly sets in. In the closed type, which can rapidly prove fatal, the symptoms are more acute, the fever is usually greater, there is no discharge and as the pus cannot escape, it is pent up within the uterus, there is considerable abdominal enlargement and the abdomen feels hard and is painful to the touch. A case of pyometra may begin as an open type and end as a closed, or *vice versa*.

Whatever its type, pyometra is a very serious and frequently fatal condition, and it requires immediate expert attention if the bitch's life is to be saved. Provided it is performed before the animal becomes too weak and toxic, an operation involving removal of the uterus and its infected contents (ovario-hysterectomy) is usually successful, but it must be carried out quickly. Mixture 1 may be given in small amounts until the bitch is seen by a veterinary surgeon (Appendix, p. 84). Where the bitch is valuable as a brood or is very old and weak, more conservative treatment may be decided upon, and this is often successful provided it is begun at an early stage, but whatever the type of pyometra, and whatever the age of the bitch, early treatment is important.

Although pyometra can appear at any time, the danger period is about 4–6 weeks from the end of the last season, and any signs of increased thirst, slight abdominal enlargement, etc., should be regarded as highly suspicious. (For Abortion, see p. 17.)

Rabies

The advance of the rabies virus, which is now a well-established disease among foxes and other wildlife in France and which is spreading towards the Channel coastline, emphasises the need for extra awareness of this killer disease, not only in relation to dogs but also to man. The quarantine regulations are strictly enforced in the UK and, unless pet-owners criminally try to import their pets into this country, these regulations are our real and only means of defence.

Rabies affects the dog by a gradual or sudden change in temperament – quiet dogs become vicious and aggressive dogs become morose and retiring. Any dog which shows unusual behaviour, especially if it has been in quarantine kennels in the previous twelve months, should be confined in an escape-proof room and a veterinary surgeon informed. Under no circumstances should the animal be handled. Hydrophobia, or the fear of water, a symptom commonly seen in infected humans, is never seen in dogs. This disease is a killer and therefore any suspected case should be attended immediately by a practising veterinary surgeon, or by a veterinary officer of the Ministry of Agriculture, Fisheries and Food.

Scalds. See Burns and Scalds, p. 24.

Shock

Shock is evidenced by a collapse of the circulation. It is usually due to internal injury, haemorrhages, poisoning, peritonitis or similar severe and serious states. In all cases of shock the animal must be attended as soon as possible by a veterinary surgeon. An animal in a state of shock is weak but usually conscious, extremities are cold, mucous membranes (e.g. gums) pale, and respirations shallow and rapid.

The animal should be placed in a warm room surrounded by rugs, blankets and hot-water bottles. Lying the animal on its right side on an electric blanket is ideal as this gives regular, equal warmth. Stimulants should not be given by mouth if there is any suspicion of internal injury, but otherwise any of the following may be given:

One teaspoonful to 1 tablespoonful (according to size) of brandy or whisky. Glucose (dissolved in a little warm milk) or any other warm milk food, e.g. Benger's, Horlicks', etc. Small amounts should be given every 5–10 minutes.

A useful mixture on such occasions, which may be administered until help arrives, is Mixture 2 (see Appendix, p. 84). Mix this together thoroughly with a whisk, then give 1 teaspoonful to 1 tablespoonful (according to size) every 15 minutes.

The animal must be kept absolutely still and quiet. If there is any vomiting following the administration by mouth of a preparation, this dosing should be stopped.

Snake Bites

Fortunately, only occasionally are dogs bitten by a snake in this country. Whilst a bite is unlikely to prove fatal to humans it can sometimes kill a small animal like a dog. The case must be treated promptly, and the animal should be seen by a veterinary surgeon as soon as possible. First-aid measures are important, and in some cases vital. Naturally they must vary with the site of the bite, and with the distance from home or help.

If the bite is on a limb, and you are some distance from home, tie a handkerchief firmly *above* the bite. This will keep the poison localised until you can take more active measures.

When at home, if possible nick the site of the bite with the corner of a razor blade, making a small cut between the fang marks. Flush this small wound thoroughly with cold water, then rub into it some potassium permanganate crystals. Do not loosen your handkerchief until after this has been done. You may then give a little glucose and water by mouth. Keep the dog warm until he has been attended by a veterinary surgeon. (For Shock, see p. 67.)

It is wise, if you live in an area where snakes are found, to carry a few antihistamine capsules or tablets with you, and a little phial containing some potassium permanganate crystals. Your veterinary surgeon will be able to give you these, and a capsule or tablet of one of these given promptly by mouth will help to minimise general poisoning from the bite.

Sores (Bed or Pressure Sores)

Thin-skinned dogs which have had a long and debilitating illness are sometimes subject to these, which are caused by pressure and congestion of the blood in the affected areas. Large, shallow, unhealthy sores appear which are sometimes very resistant to treatment. If a bed sore is noticed a veterinary surgeon should be consulted. In the meantime, zinc ointment spread on lint and bandaged on the parts, or boracic powder thickly sprinkled over the sore and a bandage applied, will do no harm as a first-aid measure.

These sores can be prevented by attention to hygiene (clean bedding), frequent turning of helpless or paralysed patients, massage with methylated spirits to harden the skin in danger areas, the protection of pressure points with cottonwool or air pillows, and general attention to comfort. Deep, soft beds are essential and if blankets are used, be careful that these are kept very smooth.

(For Paralysis, see p. 54.)

Stings (Anaphylaxis, Urticaria)

Stings are common in the summer months, and are of course acutely painful. They are usually caused by wasps, bees or hornets, and the usual site of their attack is in the mouth, owing to the dog snapping at the insect. The animal shows extreme discomfort, scratching and pawing at the mouth and salivating profusely.

The mouth or area stung should be thoroughly bathed with a solution of bicarbonate of soda made up in tepid or warm water. A concentration of 1 tablespoonful of household bicarbonate to 1–2 pints of water should be used; this is quite harmless if swallowed. Ordinary washing soda may be used instead; in this case the sting area may be wiped with a crystal of this, or a solution of 1 teaspoonful to ½ pint of warm water may be applied. The bathing should continue for at least 5 minutes and can be repeated every 10 minutes or so until the irritation has subsided. Ammoniated quinine applied sparingly will also be found effective. For excitable dogs it is wise to give 5–10 gr. potassium bromide or similar sedative as this will help to quieten the animal. In the case of bee stings it may be possible to remove the hair-like sting with forceps.

If veterinary help is within a reasonable distance it is as well to have the animal examined as soon as the initial bathing has been done. An injection of one of the recently developed antihistamines will greatly relieve the local irritation and swelling. It will also prevent any systemic disturbances. These drugs may also be given by mouth, and if there are large numbers of wasp nests in the vicinity, and stings are common occurrences, it is advisable to contact your veterinary surgeon and obtain an antihistamine for future use. This can then be given immediately following a sting, but the local bathing should not be neglected.

The above remarks apply also to urticaria (nettle rash) except, of course, that the areas affected are usually greater and the degree of irritation not so severe. Caladryl (Parke Davis) is an ideal preparation to treat this as it also contains an antihistamine. Alternatively, cortisone ointments may be presented.

Temperature, How to Take

A half-minute short-bulbed clinical thermometer is necessary. See that the mercury is well shaken down to 32°C (90°F). The bulb of the thermometer should be lightly greased with vaseline and gently inserted into the rectum for about two inches. A restless animal can be held by an assistant. Keep the instrument in position for a full minute, withdraw, wipe with cottonwool dipped in antiseptic, and read the scale. A dog's temperature is best taken when he has been resting for half an hour. When the thermometer is in daily use (during an illness, for example) it should be kept in a little glass jar – the kind used for meat pastes is suitable – with a little cottonwool at the bottom, and diluted antiseptic. Be careful the latter is not too strong as it can affect the marking on the instrument. Never use hot water for washing, and wipe or flush the antiseptic off before inserting the thermometer into the dog's rectum.

Temperature, Variations in

The normal temperature of a dog is higher than the human – roughly 38.5°C (101.5°F). Variations are, however, perfectly possible in health, and some have a temperature as low as 38°C (100°F). Puppies tend to run higher normal temperatures than adults and an excitable dog may have a slight temperature for an hour or two even when perfectly well.

When a dog looks listless, and refuses his food, the temperature should always be taken. If it is over 39°C (102.5°F) the veterinary surgeon should be informed. It may be nothing at all, but so often the virus diseases such as hard-pad and distemper begin in a very insidious way, so one cannot be too careful. Again, the temperature should be taken daily for a week after whelping. There is often a slight rise and of this no notice needs to be taken, but if it rises to 39.5°C (103°F) or over, and the bitch seems shivery and disinclined for food, the veterinary surgeon must be told at once. Possibly a dead puppy or afterbirth has not been expelled and, if retained, it can be the cause of septicaemia in a very short time. (See Placenta, p. 57.)

During illness the temperature should be taken at least twice daily, at the same times if possible, and the result written down. This is most important as the variations in temperature in some diseases and conditions are of great significance.

Any rise over about 39°C (102.5°F) can be regarded as fever. Slight fever (or mild pyrexia) is 39–39.5°C (102.5–103.5°F), fever from 39.5–40.5°C (103.5–104.5°F) and high fever (or hyperpyrexia) from 40.5°C (104.5°F) upwards. Sometimes slight fever, particularly in hard-pad, is more dangerous than a higher one. A very high temperature – 41–41.5°C (105.5–106.5°F) – should never be ignored and, apart from the treatment given for the disease of which the high temperature is merely a symptom, some attempt must be made to reduce it. This can usually be done by ice packs (see Concussion, p. 26), Paracetamol tablets, and plenty of fluids, but the veterinary surgeon treating the case may suggest some other measure.

A sub-normal temperature can be, in some instances, more

dangerous than a high fever. After specific treatment in the virus diseases the temperature occasionally drops to 37.5°C (99°F) or so, but no notice need be taken provided the animal is kept warm. The temperature in cases of shock and collapse is usually very low – 36–37°C (97–98.5°F) or so – and in cases of internal haemorrhage – an occasional and disquieting phenomenon in leptospiral jaundice and contagious hepatitis – the temperature can drop even lower, and the patient is severely collapsed with blanched mucous membranes. A fatal outcome is common in such cases. Treatment should be as described for shock (see p. 67) but a veterinary surgeon will normally have been consulted.

Temperatures usually drop gradually to normal in the course of a few days or weeks, although they may rise again after a short intermission. (This is typical in distemper when, after a brief initial period of fever, the temperature returns to normal for about a week, then rises again.) When the fall is gradual it is termed a fall by 'lysis', but when (as sometimes happens) it is rapid and dramatic within twenty-four hours or less it is known as a 'crisis'. In the old days, before the antibiotics and sulpha drugs were known, the high temperature in pneumonia cases in humans often ended by a crisis.

Fever must not be looked upon as an unmitigated evil. It shows that the body is putting up a strong resistance to the harmful infection causing the disease.

Even when the temperature returns to normal it should be taken daily for a week in case of a relapse, when it will rise again.

Thorns in Pads

This minor mishap occurs frequently with dogs whose lives are not bounded by an asphalt road or concrete pavement. It is only minor in nature, like a blister on a human foot, and if dealt with promptly and sensibly the incident is soon forgotten. Look carefully at the pads as soon as the dog begins to limp or licks at his foot. If this is done the thorn will often be seen intact, its point embedded in the pad. Carefully grasp the stout end of the thorn and pull it out, taking care not to break it. When at home once more, bathe the foot thoroughly with warm water, dry, then dab with tincture of iodine. No further attention should be necessary.

If, however, the thorn has broken, leaving only the sharp point in the pad, a good light, a sharp pair of eyes, and a pair of forceps are the most successful combination. Removal will have to be done at home, but little damage is likely to happen on the way as the dog will 'carry' the tender limb. Fine pointed forceps are ideal, but depilatory (eyebrow plucking) forceps are quite useful. When the thorn has been removed dab the point of entry with a little iodine.

When, despite a thorough search, no sign of the thorn can be found soak the foot thoroughly in warm water, gently washing the pads at the same time sometimes a small crack or cut, or split, may be the cause of the pain, and minute granules of glass, dirt or sand getting lodged in these small wounds cause quite a tender foot. This bathing should be repeated twice daily until the pain has gone.

If after 2 or 3 days there is any swelling, heat or pain it is as well to consult your veterinary surgeon. The foreign body may have worked right into the fleshy portion of the pad and produced a small abscess. This will have to be opened under local anaesthetic, and then probed and cleansed to remove the cause of the trouble.

Generally speaking, however, the thorn in the pad case is one which the owner can usually deal with quite adequately. (For Pads, Cracked, see p. 54.)

Ticks

Ticks are sometimes a cause of extreme irritation to dogs. They are oval in shape and grey or brown in colour, and about ¼″ long, being much larger than the more common parasites, fleas or lice. Ticks are most frequently acquired by dogs in the autumn months, especially if the dogs have been on land recently pastured with sheep. The tick is a blood-sucker and buries its head, which has very powerful jaws, into the dog's skin. The rear portion of the tick lies free of the skin, and when touched gives the impression that the parasite is only lightly adhering to the animal. Any attempt to pull the body of the tick will result in the body coming away, leaving the head and jaw portion firmly embedded in the skin. If this happens, the irritation caused by the remaining head will result in a painful area. A small abscess may form.

To remove the tick in its entirety is therefore most important, and this can be managed by making the parasite relax its hold on the animal. This is best done by holding a swab of cottonwool, well soaked in methylated spirit, surgical spirit, ether or chloroform, over the tick for a good 3–5 minutes. The spirit must come into direct contact with the head, so the dog's hair should be parted at the tick's point of attachment. It is important that the spirit-soaked swab is pressed firmly on the tick to ensure adequate penetration of the anaesthetising fluid. After this thorough soaking the body of the tick should be grasped and a firm, gentle tug should remove it intact. The small wound caused by the tick should be well swabbed with a little tincture of iodine, and this dressing repeated each day for two days.

Vagina, Discharge from

This is quite common, even in health, and there is, of course, the periodic flow of blood seen in the 'in season' bitch. Maiden bitches often have a slight yellow discharge and provided this remains scanty, and the bitch is well in herself, there is no need to worry.

It is normal for a bitch to have a discharge after whelping, but this usually dries up in a couple of weeks or so. When it persists for four weeks or longer veterinary advice is advisable. Such a discharge may be weakening and could be associated with a low-grade local infection. *Excessive* haemorrhage after whelping may be due to lacerations resulting from a difficult birth. Whatever the cause, professional attention is needed.

A slight greenish vaginal discharge, *unaccompanied by any other symptoms*, is probably due to some localised infection. If it persists it should be reported; it may be due to streptococcal or staphylococcal infection which can cause 'missing' in mated bitches or 'fading out' of puppies. This infection, which is fairly common, is usually amenable to treatment by a veterinary surgeon, but as it is contagious it should be treated as soon as possible.

When the discharge is offensive, brown or greenish in appearance, and there is a rise in temperature to 39.5°C (103°F) or over, immediate veterinary assistance should be sought. In a mated bitch it may mean one or more dead puppies or, after whelping, a dead puppy which has not been expelled, or a retained placenta (see p. 57).

With pyometra (see p. 65) a pinkish or brownish vaginal discharge occurs about 4 to 6 weeks after the season in elderly bitches (usually maidens). This, too, requires immediate veterinary attention.

Sometimes a bitch seems perpetually in season, with or without the coloured discharge, but when mated she has no puppies, although she is very keen. Such a condition (known as nymphomania) is usually due to ovarian cysts. The ovaries may be surgically removed but as this naturally precludes breeding many veterinary surgeons prefer to try hormone treatment. Sometimes this is successful; the bitch resumes her normal oestral cycle and can then be mated with a reasonable chance of producing puppies. Hormone treatment is likely to succeed only if the cysts are not very large, so obviously there must be prompt professional consultation if this condition is suspected.

To sum up: if a vaginal discharge is slight, it can usually be ignored if the animal is otherwise well. If excessive, offensive, or abnormal in any way a veterinary surgeon should be consulted, and if in addition the bitch is feverish and refusing her food it is a matter of some urgency.

Unless otherwise advised, the parts should be kept clean with warm water. If swabs are to be taken to test for the presence of a streptococcal infection the parts should not be touched and no antiseptic preparation used.

Vomiting

This is a common symptom in many diseases – gastritis, nephritis, pyometra, etc. – or it can be purely transitory (for example, travel sickness or over-eating). The cause should be found and dealt with. Withholding food for a few hours can do no harm if the cause is over-eating. In other cases, white of egg and milk should be given by mouth, or Mixture 1 in the Appendix, (p. 84). This helps to soothe the inflamed digestive organs. Vomiting is often accompanied by thirst, and water should be withheld, barley water, flat soda water or ice to lick being substituted. During convalescence Brand's Essence, Complan, Benger's Food and similar preparations are easily assimilated and put no strain on the digestive system.

Except in mild cases, it is wise to obtain veterinary advice as vomiting, if frequent, is often a symptom of some serious disorder.

Whelping

Whilst the natural process of birth is in no way an emergency, and if normal does not require any assistance or first-aid measures, a number of variations of, or from, the normal may arise. Some of these may amount to actual abnormality and need professional attendance, or perhaps assistance from the owner. The following comments are intended to help the inexperienced to distinguish between normal and abnormal, between the natural physiological process and pathological complications. Even quite experienced breeders often find this aspect of whelping difficult to grasp. The uncertainty of risking the puppies' lives and the danger of harm to the bitch, creates a large problem in their minds. Generally speaking, it is better to consult your veterinary surgeon too early rather than to delay too long as the chance of survival of mother and young will then be proportionally greater. If surgical interference is necessary it is the fit animal which will stand the best chances, not the exhausted bitch. Any surgical action which is required should be left strictly to the veterinary surgeon; on no account should the owner attempt, or permit anyone else to attempt, delivery by the use of forceps, etc.

The first signs of parturition are restlessness, 'bed-making', and often, refusal of food. There is usually a marked fall in body temperature to about 37°C (98°F) twenty-four hours or so before whelping. Shivering and panting are usual, and these signs are all quite normal. Within several hours of the beginning of these symptoms actual labour will begin. The contractions of the womb or uterus will start and at this stage the bitch will show signs of periodic acute discomfort, heaving, straining and panting. These spasms will become more frequent and sustained as the whelping process goes on. It is important to note the time when the first real labour pains (i.e. straining) are seen as much depends on the intervals between beginning of symptoms and appearance, or non-appearance, of puppies.

The first thing that is noticed in a normal whelping is the water bag, which may be seen only as a sudden expulsion of fluid, as it ruptures, or is ruptured by the bitch. If this sign has not been seen after 1 *hour* from time of labour it is wise to make sure that all is going well. This can be done only by a vaginal examination with a well-scrubbed and soaped finger. Gently insert the finger into the vagina, and the puppy should be felt in the pelvic cavity, i.e. within a few inches of the vulva. Do not push or probe about if the puppy can be felt. Leave the bitch for 15–20 minutes; then, if no puppy has been born, re-examine the bitch. If the puppy has not moved further down towards the vulva, or if at the first examination no puppy or water bag could be felt, call your veterinary surgeon. These time limits are conservative; some bitches are slower than this but are nevertheless quite normal. Generally speaking, however, the time limits stated should not be greatly exceeded. The first puppy is usually followed within 20 minutes–1 hour by the second, and so on until the whole litter has arrived. The bitch may rest for a few minutes after having, say, 2 or 3 puppies, and of course this time should not be counted when deciding how matters are going. A little (1–4 tablespoonsful) of Mixture 2 (see Appendix, p. 84) may be given at this stage, but no solid food, and at the conclusion of the whelping. Complications are therefore best assessed by judging the time delays involved, supplemented when necessary by gentle vaginal exploration.

One complication, *uterine inertia*, is seen occasionally. If this is suspected your veterinary surgeon should be informed straight away.

This takes two main forms:

(*a*) The bitch will go through all the routine of bed-making, etc., and then, after a little abdominal discomfort, show no further signs of labour or uterine contractions. This is known as primary uterine inertia.

(*b*) The bitch may show signs of straining, often quite good to begin with but becoming weaker and fewer, without the appearance of the puppy. This is called secondary uterine inertia. Both these types of uterine inertia require skilled attention, which may or may not involve surgical assistance. One of the predisposing causes of uterine inertia, or 'going to sleep on the job', is over-fatness, and bitches should be kept in a fit, properly exercised state right up to the actual day of whelping. Certain medical conditions also predispose or cause this lack of uterine tone, but search for the cause and the necessary treatment should be left to the expert.

Attention to Puppies

Puppies will not usually require attention from the owner of a normal bitch, who has whelped successfully by herself. However, in short-nosed breeds, e.g. Pekingese, King Charles Spaniels and English Bulldogs, it is sometimes necessary to attend to the umbilical cord, if the puppy is born intact, or attached to the foetal sac (or 'puppy-bag') as the membranes in which the puppy lies when in the womb are called. The cord should be tied off about ¼"–½" from the puppy's navel with sterile cotton (i.e. boiled cotton) and the membrane or 'bag' side of the cord cut with sterilised scissors. The stump should then be dabbed with a little tincture of iodine.

Lifeless Puppies

Occasionally a puppy that has been delayed in birth does not gasp when born. The mouth should be opened with a finger and the spine given a brisk rubbing with a dry towel. A little cold water on the nape of the neck will help to stimulate a reflex inspiration. If mucus is in the mouth wipe this away with a little moistened cottonwool and blow sharply into the opened mouth. A *drop* of brandy on the tongue will also produce a reflex inhalation and is a useful stimulant for a weakly pup. When the puppy is breathing regularly, *but not before*, place him on a towel or blanket, near a hot-water bottle. A drop of brandy may be given every 20–30 minutes until he can be suckled by the bitch. See also Puppies, deaths in the newborn (p. 64).

Whelping, Diet After

There is no need nowadays to give liquid diet after whelping provided the temperature is normal. A light diet should be given such as boiled fish for a day or two, then chicken or rabbit, followed by raw meat. A nursing bitch should be well fed as the puppies are a big drain on her strength. She should have from three to five meals a day, depending on the size of the litter – milk to begin with, with or without porridge – brown bread, gravy, raw meat (about six ounces for a 12 kilo (30 lb) dog), Stress and halibut oil for dinner, and raw meat (six to eight ounces for Fox Terrier size) for supper. The two additional meals when required could consist of paunch, fish or beaten-up egg in milk for one meal, and a bowl of warm milk last thing at night for the other. The allocation of raw meat should be generous, particularly if the litter is a large one. Such a diet should ensure a plentiful supply of milk and the bitch should be in excellent physical condition, even after rearing a large litter, if fed on the lines suggested.

Worms. See Diarrhoea (p. 27).

Wounds

These fall into four principal categories: incised (when there is a clean cut, as from a knife), lacerated (when the skin and other parts are torn), contused (when bruising is also present) and punctured (when the wound is small and deep, as when caused by a sharp-pointed instrument or a dog's tooth). For contused wounds see Bruises (p. 23), and for punctured wounds see Bites (p. 21) and Abscesses (p. 18). The care of smaller skin wounds will be dealt with here.

As a preliminary to dealing with any wound, however small, always wash your hands.

When a small injury is badly contaminated with dirt and matted with dried blood these must first be removed, using plain warm boiled water only, in order to see the extent of the wound. Some injuries which appear very bad will be found to be quite minor after receiving this preliminary cleaning up.

Carefully remove the hair for about an inch round the wound and, in a long-haired dog, shorten any hair near it so that it cannot fall across the surface. Nail scissors (the straight kind) will be found useful for removing the hair round the edges of the wound, but be careful that hair does not enter the wound. Examine the cut or injury and if there are any loose shreds of skin, hair, or other foreign matter in the wound itself remove them with forceps previously sterilised by boiling for two minutes. The forceps will also be useful in examining the wound if it is at all deep. Always work with great gentleness and smoothness, never jabbing or prodding, and be as speedy as efficiency permits. Bathe the wound carefully with warm water and Dettol (one tea-spoonful to the pint) using gentle, sweeping strokes and not dabbing or rubbing. Use each piece of cottonwool once only and wipe *away* from the injury. Do *not* apply ointment of any kind.

Most wounds are better left unbandaged unless large in extent (when they should receive veterinary attention) or where they can be contaminated – for example, the foot.

Household disinfectants should never be used for bathing wounds as they are usually poisonous or too strong. Dettol makes a useful antiseptic, properly diluted, for dogs. TCP is also useful as a mild antiseptic. Alternatively a saline solution can be used (one large tea-spoonful of salt to a pint of boiled water).

The subsequent dressing of the wound will depend on its type and gravity but, broadly speaking, the less injuries are touched the better, after the initial cleansing. The tissues must have time to heal, and con-stant swabbing with even the mildest antiseptic is not advisable as sepsis is most unlikely to occur if the wound has been properly treated in the first place. It should be inspected daily but not touched unless there is any discharge. Once the wound is clean, subsequent blood clots and scabs need not be removed if clean in appearance, as they protect the injury. This does *not* apply to wounds of a deeply penetrat-ing type, which must be kept open for free drainage. As long as the injury looks healthy and is drying up and the skin around a normal colour, all is well. With sepsis the skin surrounding the place is red-dened and inflamed, the wound is either closed or partially so, there may or may not be considerable discharge, and the edges of the wound will be swollen, red, shiny and unhealthy-looking. Such cases are, however, extremely rare as the average small, shallow wound heals with remarkable rapidity if properly treated.

When the skin is badly torn, or the cut longer than about an inch, it will need more elaborate treatment and suturing by a veterinary sur-geon. Such cases are better not dressed by the owner as damage can easily be caused by unskilled handling. Dirt or other contamination can be gently removed with boiled water and the surface of the injury protected by a piece of lint and a bandage until the animal can be attended to by a veterinary surgeon. In the case of a cut requiring suturing, the lips of the wound should be brought together as closely as possible before applying the lint and the bandaging should be firm in order to keep the wound to some extent closed. (For bleeding, see Haemorrhage, p. 41.)

4

Recent Advances in Veterinary Surgery

The past decades have been a period of continuing advances in the art and science of veterinary surgery. Even the last few years have seen advances of outstanding value. In the field of surgery, operations are carried out today which a few years ago could not have been contemplated. Operations into the chest cavity or intra-thoracic surgery involving such vital organs as the gullet and lungs and heart are now accessible to the surgeon's skill. The 'pinning' of bones, where the old-fashioned and cumbersome splint has gone by the board, has resulted in finer and more rapid repair, with far less pain and discomfort to the patient. Prostatectomy, or removal of the prostate gland which causes so much trouble in the older male dog, has now become a possibility and is one of the conditions to come within the scope of the surgeon. Safer anaesthetics have reduced the hazards of surgery very considerably.

For the clinicians the antibiotics have greatly widened the horizons of veterinary medicine. The newer antibiotics have a broad spectrum activity which means that they are effective against a very wide range of disease-producing organisms. Virus diseases have still to be conquered by antibiotics or chemotherapeutic agents, but their life too is limited. The newer antibiotics have also the added advantage of being less weakening or harmful to the patient and thus enable a more rapid recovery. The fact that many are effective when given by mouth means that the patient can often be nursed successfully at home and suffer less disturbance as a result.

For the aged patient the cortisone group of drugs have resulted in a great saving of both life and also discomfort. In cases of eye damage or disease, this group of drugs has saved the sight of hundreds of animals which before would have become blind, or even have died.

Anaesthesia, widely used as a routine in all surgical measures, is today safer than it ever has been. Muscle relaxants and tranquillisers have meant that lower dosages of general anaesthetics can be employed, resulting in less risk to the animal at time of surgery and a more speedy recovery afterwards, because the degree of surgical shock has been reduced.

In the realm of the virus diseases, whilst no chemotherapeutic agent has been developed which is specifically effective against this ultra-microscopic group of organisms, more anti-sera and vaccines are available than ever before to combat these diseases, and it is up to the individual dog owner to make full use of these valuable assets to prevent rather than try to cure such diseases. Distemper and Rubarth's disease (contagious hepatitis) are the two main ones in this group of virus infections.

All this means in terms of the individual dog that not only has much of the pain, misery and disfigurement been removed from cases of accident or disease, but also that a dog which would previously have had to be euthanased can now frequently be saved to lead a normal or near normal life.

In the field of bone surgery, antibiotics have enabled the surgeon to enlarge his scope to deal successfully with almost every kind of bone injury. In the past bone surgery has been handicapped by the constant menace of infection at the time of injury, and bones having a poor blood supply are particularly prone to become centres of infection, once contaminated.

The X-ray photographs (between pages 44 and 45) show how a completely shattered limb can be reconstructed using a stainless steel pin as a foundation, resulting in a new life for the animal. Surgery such as this not only requires a high degree of technical skill, making use of all the aids available, but also a sustained attack on the bacteria which are liable to have entered the skin wound in such cases of compound fracture. These antibiotic 'umbrellas', as they are called, are of the greatest value to the surgeon, and many can be given by mouth, which means more rest for the convalescent patient. In the post-operative period, just as during the actual operation, new drugs of the tranquilliser type provide a safer and more restful convalescence. These agents can be employed for long periods and do not have the depressing side effects found with the earlier barbiturate group of preparations. In addition, these tranquillisers may be used in conjunction with the true hypnotics, but the dosage rates of these more dangerous drugs may be reduced accordingly.

Plastics are today beginning to play an increasingly important rôle in veterinary surgery. In cases of joint or bone injury new bones can be built up with these new compounds (see photograph of greyhound between pages 44 and 45). The advantages of such new agents are that they are light, unlike stainless steel, and being non-irritant to the tissues with which they are in contact, they can be left *in situ* permanently. Plastics have also aided the surgeon in the field of sutures. Stitches using nylon, available in all its many versatile forms, are everyday practice in wound surgery. Nylon has the advantages of being easily sterilised (unlike cat-gut), it is light and does not hold bacteria like silk or older types of suture materials.

. Advances in the treatment of shock, that old and ever-present enemy of the surgeon, are many. Transfusions, using whole blood or artificial blood volume expanders, are now used each day in veterinary practice. Shock is a constant risk in any type of surgery, but particularly in cases of injury, where there is a severe loss of blood, or in the aged patient. Transfusions, safer anaesthetics and other specific anti-shock treatment has greatly reduced the losses from this highly dangerous sequel to any injury.

Today it is true to say that the dogs in the United Kingdom are healthier than they ever have been. Distemper and many of the other infectious or contagious diseases have been controlled most effectively by the widespread use of effective and safe vaccines. These vaccines have undoubtedly contributed very greatly to freeing the dog owner from many of the worries and many of the risks which he was placed at in the past and their continued use by educated dog owners will no doubt make sure that this happy state will continue.

However at a time when we are able to be satisfied that distemper and other diseases are well under control in the United Kingdom, the dog population is about to be placed in greater risk probably than it has ever been before This refers to the very real risk of rabies becoming a condition affecting dogs and other animals in this country. The risk is all too near and all too great, as the continent of Europe has recently been experiencing an increased incidence of this dread disease. Our quarantine laws and regulations have been for many decades a most effective barrier through which only on very rare occasions has the occasional case of rabies slipped. However with modern transport and with a greater movement of animals than there ever has been before, then it is all too easy for the ignorant to try to smuggle animals through the ports and airports or by other means and try to avoid the authorities who are enforcing these regulations. Such lunacy, for lunacy it is, deserves nothing but severe penalties when such cases are found.

Today, the full force of the law has been mobilised to penalise heavily the foolish people who attempt to introduce animals into the country illegally. Imprisonment and hefty fine are frequently applied to such individuals who will find that ignorance of the regulations is no excuse for their stupid and dangerous actions. To place the lives of fellow human beings at risk by attempting to smuggle or introduce a pet, however much loved, into this country will only bring down the full weight of the law on their heads. The education not only of visitors from abroad, but also of British folk travelling abroad, has been a major task, but multi-lingual posters, both here and abroad, vividly proclaim the risks of introducing rabies into the British Isles and the very severe penalties which will be incurred by anyone even attempting to carry out such an act of pure recklessness.

The main risk is in the natural vectors of this disease carrying it to the United Kingdom and we have to look to our defences against these risks as well as the obvious ones of animals being smuggled in illegally.

Rabies is undoubtedly one of the most serious of the zoonotic diseases, producing as it does hydrophobia in Man. All measures must be taken to keep this country in the fortunate state that it has been, by constant surveillance and by strict application of sensible regulations. Undoubtedly one of the most important of these measures is the awareness by members of the public of the very real risks of allowing animals illegal entry into this country. It is also important that our scientists and those responsible for maintaining the 'rabies free state' of this country should be aware and look into the methods and measures which can be taken to stop the more natural and more difficult to control methods of infection being introduced into our native population of wild animals.

Fortunately reasonably effective vaccines are available against rabies, but this is a second line of defence and must be regarded as such. That we have this second line of defence is indeed fortunate but to have a country which is free of rabies where people can own animals without running the dread risk of becoming infected with this disease from them, then this is surely the criterion at which to aim – not only now, but always.

The wonders of modern therapeutics and surgery are unfolding year by year and today the injured or sick animal stands a better chance of recovery than ever before. As a result of all the many aspects of research going on at this moment, the dog of the future will be able to look upon man as the best friend he ever had. Even then, and even more so today, there is still the ever constant need for good care and nursing; for the skilled care in handling the injured or convalescent patient; for the constant alertness and meticulous attention to detail in carrying out treatment. It is our hope that this short book will have done something towards giving an insight into this, and the more specialised art of veterinary surgery.

Appendix

Mixture 1
>White of egg.
>¼ pint of skimmed milk
>1 dessertspoonful brandy
>1 tablespoonful glucose

Mixture 2
>2 whole eggs
>½ pint milk (whole)
>1 tablespoonful brandy
>1 tablespoonful glucose

Mixture 3
>1 tablespoonful water
>1 teaspoonful brandy
>1 teaspoonful sodium bicarbonate (baking soda)

Brandy is disliked by some dogs and may be omitted in such cases.

Arrowroot Gruel

Mix heaped dessertspoonful arrowroot to a thin paste with cold water. Heat ½ pint of milk (without cream) or water to boiling point. Add about 1 dessertspoonful of sugar. Then add the arrowroot paste. Stir thoroughly.

Dressings

¼ pint of *boiled* warm water, preferably in a sterilised container.

Antiphlogistine or Kaolin Poultice
These two preparations are very similar in composition, and one may be substituted for the other.

To prepare for use. Ease the lid of the tin, then place in a saucepan of convenient size, partially filled with water. The water should come about halfway up the outside of the tin containing the poultice. Warm the water slowly and allow the poultice to remain immersed for 3–5 minutes. The poultice may then be spread on the bandage or lint to be used, using a knife or spatula. A *layer* of poultice about the thickness of a thick spread of butter on bread is sufficient. When this can be comfortably borne on the back of the hand apply to the animal's skin, bandage or lint side down. Always apply the poultice cold rather than too hot as dogs have very tender skins.

Castor Oil for Eyes
Pour 1–2 teaspoonsful into a clean eggcup or similar small vessel, or a clean bottle. Stand for 2–3 minutes in warm water, and when the oil is at about blood heat apply as required.

Sedatives
Veganin, Cogene, APC tablets. Codeine Co. tablets. Potassium bromide tablets. Syrup of chloral.

All tablets are best given crushed into a powder and mixed or dissolved in a little milk.

Dosages
½–2 Veganin (according to size of dog), e.g. 12 kilo (30 lb) dog 1 tablet.

3–10 gr. bromide (according to size of dog), e.g. 12 kilo (30 lb) dog 5 gr.

These dosages may be repeated every 1½–2 hours or earlier if necessary.

Index

abdominal pain, 14–17, 59
abortion, 17–18
abscesses, 18–19, 21, 22, 72
accidental matings *see* mésalliance
accidents, 19–20
'acid milk', 64
Adexolin drops, 65
afterbirth, retained, 57–8, 70, 73
All-Bran, 15
ammonia, 43, 44
ammoniated quinine, 69
anaesthesia, 23, 39, 40, 80–1
anal sphincter, 39
antibiotics, 18, 22, 40, 53, 80, 81
antihistamine, 68, 69
antiphlogistine poultices, 19, 85
APC tablets, 85
arrowroot, 30, 61, 84
arsenic poisoning, 59, 62
arterial haemorrhage, 42
artificial respiration, 20–1
asphyxiation, 25
auto-intoxication, paralysis, 55

bacteria: diarrhoea, 27, 28; food
    poisoning, 60, 61
bandages: cracked pads, 54; ears,
    30–1; haemorrhages, 42; splinting
    fractures, 41
barbiturates, 62, 63, 81
barium chloride poisoning, 59, 62
barley haws, in eyes, 34
barley water, 24, 47, 74
bathing, feet, 72
bed sores, 10, 68
beds and bedding, 8–9; after surgery,
    52; bed sores, 68; collapsible cages,
13; fur fabric, 13
bee stings, 68–9
Benger's Food, 46, 67, 74
bicarbonate of soda, 15, 24, 69
biscuits, 47
bitches: eclampsia, 31–3; lack of milk,
    49–50; mastitis, 47–9; mésalliance,
    49; pyometra, 65–6, 73, 74; vaginal
    discharges, 73–4; whelping, 11, 13,
    74–6
bites: abscesses, 18; cat, 22; dog, 21–2;
    rat, 22; snake, 67–8
Bitter Apple, 13
bladder, incontinence, 55
blankets, 8–9
bleeding *see* haemorrhage
blindness, phenol poisoning, 60
blood transfusions, 82
bones: choking on, 25–6; as foreign
    bodies, 37–9; fractures, 39–41;
    pinning, 40, 80, 81; surgery, 81
boracic ointment, 54
boracic powder, 34, 65, 68
brain, inflammation, 23
Brand's Essence, 28, 46, 74
brandy: after gas poisoning, 60;
    artificial respiration, 21; for collapse,
    26; for colic, 15; and food poisoning,
    61; after heart attacks, 43; and heat-
    stroke, 44; for hysteria, 45; in invalid
    diet, 47; lifeless puppies, 76; for
    shock, 67
bread, 47, 52, 77
breathing, artificial respiration, 20–1
bromide, potassium of, 32, 45, 85
bronchitis kettles, 46
bruising, 23–4
burns, 24–5

cages, collapsible, 8, 13
Caladryl, 69
calcium, eclampsia, 32–3
calculi, renal, 16
canine parvovirus (CPV), 56–7
carbolic poisoning, 60, 62
case histories, 11
castor oil, 28, 34, 35, 38, 61, 85
cat bites, 22
catarrhal infections, 45
charcoal, 28, 61
chemicals, food poisoning, 60, 61
chicken, diet after whelping, 77
chloral, syrup of, 85
chloroform, 72
choking, 25–6
cleanliness, 10; puppy kennels, 27;
    sick-rooms, 8; wounds, 77–8
coal gas poisoning, 60, 62
coal tar poisoning, 60, 62
coats: pneumonia jackets, 8, 58;
    surgical, 53
cod liver oil and malt, 11, 52
codeine, 85
coffee, as stimulant, 47, 63
Cogene, 85
colic, 15
collapse, 26
collars, 5–6
Collovet, 11
Collis Brown's mixture, 28
Complan, 74
compound fractures, 39–40, 41
compresses, warm, 24
concussion, 26
constipation, 15, 33, 55
contagious hepatitis, 16–17, 71, 81
controlling dogs, 5–6, 19
convalescence, 11, 47, 52–4
convulsions *see* fits
cornea, ulceration, 34
cornflakes, 46, 47
cortisone, 69, 80
cottonwool swabs, 53
cracked pads, 54
crisis, fevers, 71
custard, baked, 46, 52
cuts *see* wounds
cysts, ovarian, 73

dehydration, 57
Dettol, 9, 10, 18, 78
dew claws, 50

diarrhoea, 27–8; canine parvovirus, 56;
    care of dog, 9–10; food poisoning,
    14, 60, 61; intussusception, 16;
    poisoning, 59
diet: after burns, 24–5; after diarrhoea,
    28; after surgery, 52–3; after
    whelping, 77; in convalescence, 11;
    and diarrhoea, 27; during a fever,
    35–6; during lactation, 49; during
    pregnancy, 32–3; hand-rearing
    puppies, 64–5; for invalids, 46–7
discharges: nasal, 50–1; vaginal, 57,
    66, 73–4
disinfectants, 78
dislocations, 29
distemper, 7, 11; and abortion, 17;
    fever, 70, 71; inhalations, 45; nasal
    discharge, 51; paralysis, 55;
    symptoms, 44; vaccinations, 81, 82
dog bites, 21–2
dosing, 29–30
douching, vagina, 49
dressings, 53–4, 78, 84–5
dysentery, 30

ears: foreign bodies in, 31; haematoma,
    31; torn, 30–1
eclampsia, 31–3
egg whites, 15, 74
eggs, 47, 52
emetics, 14, 59
encephalitis, 23
endocrine deficiencies, abortion, 17
enemas, 15, 33, 39, 55
enteritis, 56, 60–1
epileptiform convulsions, 32
Epsom salts, 15, 48, 55, 61, 63
ether, 72
eucalyptus, 45
examination, vaginal, 75
exercise, 11, 52
eyes: castor oil treatment, 85; cortisone
    treatment, 80; extrusion of eye-ball,
    34–5; eye lotions, 34; foreign bodies
    in, 34; injuries, 33–5; scratches, 34

false pregnancy, 47
Farex, 46
feet: broken nails, 50; cracked pads,
    54; dislocated toes, 29; thorns in
    pads, 71–2
feline panleucopaenia, 56
femoral artery, pulse, 10

fever *see* temperature
fights, separating dogs, 36
'figure of eight' nose tie, 6
fish, 47, 52, 77
fits: distemper, 7, 11; eclampsia, 32; hysteria, 44–5; inflammation of the brain, 23; strychnine poisoning, 59, 63
foetal sac, 64, 76
fomentations, 18, 19
food poisoning, 14, 60–1, 62
forceps, 53, 71–2, 78
foreign bodies, 36–9; in ears, 31; in eyes, 34; in gullet, 37–8; in intestines, 38–9; in mouth, 37; in nose, 50–1; in pads, 72; in rectum, 39; in stomach, 38; swallowed, 14, 15
foster-mothers, 48, 64
fractures, 39–41; compound, 39–40, 41; multiple, 39, 40–1; simple, 39, 40–1
Friar's Balsam, 45
fur fabric beds, 9, 13

gas, poisoning, 60, 62
gastritis, 14, 38, 74
glucose, 17, 35–6, 46, 52, 58, 64, 67
glycerine, 33
goat's milk, 64
grass seeds, 31, 34, 51
grooming, 8
gullet, foreign bodies in, 37–8

haematoma, 31
haemorrhage, 41–2; abortion, 17; after whelping, 73; arterial, 42; internal, 71; shock, 67; stopping, 20; venous, 42
halibut oil, 33, 52, 77
hand-rearing puppies, 64–5
handling dogs, 5–6, 19
hard-pad, 7, 11; and abortion, 17; diet during, 36; fever, 70; nasal discharge, 50, 51; paralysis, 55; symptoms, 27, 44; *see also* brain, inflammation of
headaches, 51
heart: canine parvovirus, 56; heart attacks, 42–3
heat-stroke, 43–4
heating, sick-rooms, 8

hepatitis, contagious, 16–17, 71, 81
herrings, 47
hip joint, dislocation, 29
histamine, 23
honey, 35, 52
Horlicks, 67
hormones: for lack of milk, 49; mésalliance, 49; ovarian cysts, 73
hornet stings, 68–9
hot-water bottles, 8, 10, 26, 55, 64, 65
hydrophobia, 67, 83
hypnotics, 81
hysterectomy, 66
hysteria, 32, 44–5

ice packs, 42, 44, 70
incontinence, 9–10, 13, 55
incontinent pads, 9
indigestion, 15, 44
inflammation of the brain, 23
inhalations, 45–6, 51
injections, 12
injuries, 16, 19–20; *see also* wounds
insect stings, 68–9
internal injuries, 20, 67
intestines: colic, 15; foreign bodies in, 38–9; intussusception, 16, 38–9
intussusception, 16, 38–9
invalids, diet for, 46–7
iodine, 71, 72, 73, 76

jaundice, leptospiral, 22, 71
joints, dislocations, 29

kaolin: kaolin and charcoal, 28; poultices, 18–19, 24, 85
kennels, 8, 27
kerosene, 61
kidney disease, 16, 23, 47

labour *see* whelping
lactation, 77; eclampsia, 31–3; lack of milk, 49–50
lancing, abscesses, 18
laxatives, 15
lead poisoning, 61, 62
leads: controlling dogs, 6, 19; separating fighting dogs, 36
leptospira canicola, 16
leptospira icterrohaemorrhagia, 22
leptospiral jaundice, 22, 71
lifeless puppies, 76

lint, 53, 54
liver, in invalid diet, 47
liver extract, 47
lysis, 71

mammary tumours, 48
mastitis, 18, 47–9
mating, mésalliance, 49
meat: choking on, 25; diet after
  whelping, 77; during lactation, 49;
  food poisoning, 60–1; hand-rearing
  puppies, 65; in invalid diet, 47, 52
medicine droppers, 65
medicines, dosing, 29–30
meningitis, 23
mésalliance, 49
metaldehyde poisoning, 63
methylated spirit, 68, 72
metritis, 17
milk: diet after whelping, 77; hand-
  rearing puppies, 64–5; in invalid
  diet,, 46–7, 52; lack of, 49–50
milk glands: mammary tumours, 48;
  mastitis, 18, 47–9
milk of magnesia, 24
mineral supplements, 11
miscarriage, 17–18
mouth: cleaning, 10; foreign bodies in,
  37; insect stings, 69
muscle relaxants, 80–1
myocardial canine parvovirus, 56
myositis, 23

nails: broken, 50; puppies, 48
nasal discharge, 50–1
nasal drops, 46, 51
nephritis, 16, 74
nettle rash, 69
nose: discharges, 50–1; foreign bodies
  in, 50–1
nose tie, 'figure of eight', 6
nostrils, cleaning, 51
nursing, 7–13
nylon sutures, 82
nymphomania, 73

obedience training, 5
obesity, 42, 76
observation, 11
oesophagus, foreign bodies in, 37–8
oestrogen, 48
olive oil, 15, 48, 49, 51

operations *see* surgery
ostermilk No. 1, 64
ovarian cysts, 73
ovario-hysterectomy, 66
over-eating, 74

pads: cracked, 54; thorns in, 71–2
paper-shavings, bedding, 8
Paracetamol, 45, 51, 70
paraffin, 15, 61
paralysis, 9, 54–6
parasites, ticks, 72–3
parvovirus, 12, 13, 56–7
pelvis, fractures, 40
penicillin, 18, 34, 40
penis, bleeding, 41, 42
peritonitis, 15, 38, 39, 57, 67
permanganate of potash, 10, 63
'phantom' pregnancy, 47
phenobarbitone, 63
phenol poisoning, 59, 60, 62
phosphorus, 33; poisoning, 62, 63
pills, how to give, 30
pine-shavings, bedding, 8
pinning bones, 80, 81
placenta, retained, 57–8, 70, 73
plastics, in surgery, 81–2
pneumonia jackets, 8, 58
poisoning, 14, 59–64; arsenic, 59, 62;
  barbiturates, 62, 63; barium chloride,
  59, 62; carbolic, 60, 62; coal gas,
  60, 62; coal tar, 60, 62; food, 60–1,
  62; lead, 61, 62; metaldehyde, 63;
  phenol, 59, 60, 62; phosphorus, 62,
  63; respiratory collapse, 20; shock,
  67; strychnine, 62, 63; Warfarin,
  63–4
porridge, 77
potash, permanganate of, 10, 63
potassium bromide, 69, 85
potassium permanganate, 68
poultices, kaolin, 18–19, 24, 85
pregnancy: abortion, 17–18; diet
  during, 32–3; false, 47; *see also*
  whelping
premature whelping, 17
pressure sores, 68
prostatectomy, 80
protein, 24–5, 49, 52–3
pulse, 10
puncture wounds, 22, 77

Index

puppies: dead, 64, 73; diarrhoea, 27;
  hysteria, 44; intussusception, 16,
  38–9; lifeless, 76; nails, 48; rearing
  by hand, 64–5; temperature, 70;
  whelping, 75, 76
'puppy-bag', 64, 76
pus, pyometra, 65–6
pyometra, 65–6, 73, 74

quarantine, 66, 82
quinine, 69

rabbit, in diet, 47, 52, 77
rabies, 66–7, 82–3
rat bites, 22
rat poisons, 59, 61, 63
rectum: foreign bodies in, 39; taking
  temperature in, 69–70
renal calculi, 16
renal pain, 16
respiration, artificial, 20–1
respiratory collapse, 20
restlessness, 14
restraining dogs, 5–6, 19
retained placenta, 57–8, 70, 73
rheumatism, 23
Rodine, 63
Rubarth's disease, 16–17, 81
rusks, 47

saline solution, 78
salmonella, 61
sardines, 47
scalds, 24–5
scratches, eyes, 34
season, 73
sedatives, 85; after accidents, 19, 20;
  eclampsia, 32; for hysteria, 45;
  inflammation of the brain, 23
sepsis, 24, 78
septicaemia, 70
shock, 24, 67, 82
sick-rooms, 8
'Sleek' plaster, 54
sleep, 7, 10
slug bait, 63
smelling-salts, 21, 43, 44
snake bites, 67–8
soapy water, enemas, 33
soda: emetics, 14, 59; for insect stings,
  69
soda water, 74

sores, bed, 68
splints, 40–1, 80
sponging, 10
Stader splints, 40
staphylococcal infection, 64, 73
sterilization, 53
stings, 68–9
stitches, 21, 78–9, 82; removal, 53–4
stomach, foreign bodies in, 38
straw bedding, 8, 9
streptococcal infection, 64, 73
streptomycin, 40
Stress (dietary supplement), 32, 47, 77
strychnine poisoning, 59, 62, 63
surgery: after-care, 52–4; recent
  advances, 80–3; removal of foreign
  bodies, 38
surgical coats, 53
surgical spirit, 72
sutures, 21, 78–9, 82; removal, 53–4
swabs, cottonwool, 53
symptoms, daily record, 11
syringes, enemas, 33

talcum powder, 9, 10
tar, poisoning, 60, 62
TCP, 51, 78
tea-chests, as beds, 8, 9
teething, hysteria, 44
temperature: abscesses, 18; after
  surgery, 54; before whelping, 75; and
  diarrhoea, 28; feeding in fevers,
  35–6; food poisoning, 61; how to
  take, 69–70; leptospira canicola, 16;
  in mastitis, 48; and nasal discharge,
  51; pyometra, 66; reducing, 10;
  retained placenta, 57; sick-rooms, 8;
  and vaginal discharge, 73; variations
  in, 70–1
Thermogene wool, 58
thermometers, 69–70
thirst, 48, 66, 74
thorns in pads, 71–2
ticks, 72–3
toes, dislocation, 29
toxaemia, 23, 24, 66
toxins, food poisoning, 60–1
toys, choking on, 25
tranquillisers, 45, 80–1
transfusions, blood, 82
travel sickness, 74
tumours, mammary, 48

umbilical cord, 76
unconsciousness, 20, 26, 43, 60
uraemia, 23
urticaria, 69
uterus: metritis, 17; pyometra, 65–6,
    73, 74; uterine inertia, 64, 75–6;
    whelping, 75

vaccination, 81, 82; canine parvovirus,
    57; leptospira, 16, 22; rabies, 83
vagina: discharges, 57, 66, 73–4;
    examination during whelping, 75
vaseline, 48, 51
Veganin, 18, 45, 85
venous haemorrhage, 42
ventilation, sick-rooms, 8
Vetbed, 13, 52
veterinary nursing, 12–13
veterinary surgeons, 11–12
virus diseases, 71, 80, 81
vitamin A, 47
vitamin B complex, 47
vitamin D, 32–3, 47
vitamin E, 17
vitamin supplements, 11, 47, 52
vomiting, 14, 74; canine parvovirus,
    56–7; foreign bodies, 38;

intussusception, 16; poisoning, 59

walking sticks: controlling dogs, 6;
    separating fighting dogs, 36
Warfarin poisoning, 63–4
warm compresses, 24
washing soda, 59, 69
wasp stings, 68–9
water bag, 75
whelping, 11, 13, 74–6; diet after, 77;
    discharges after, 73; eclampsia,
    31–3; fever after, 70; pain, 15;
    premature, 17; retained placenta,
    57–8; signs of, 75; uterine inertia,
    64, 75–6; whelping beds, 64
whisky, for shock, 67
worms: diarrhoea, 27; hysteria, 44;
    worming, 17
wounds, 77–9; bites, 21–2; cleaning,
    77–8; dressings, 53–4; first aid, 19;
    stitches, 78–9; stopping bleeding, 42

X-rays: bone surgery, 81; dislocations,
    29; foreign bodies, 37, 38; fractures,
    40; renal calculi, 16

zinc ointment, 9, 10, 68